WRITING POEMS p

MICHAEL HARRISON AND CHRISTOPHER STUAR

OXFORD UNIVERSITY PRESS 1992

Oxford University Press, Walton Street, Oxford OX2 6DP

Oxford New York Toronto
Delhi Bombay Calcutta Madras Karachi
Petaling Jaya Singapore Hong Kong Tokyo
Nairobi Dar es Salaam Cape Town
Melbourne Auckland

and associated companies in
Berlin Ibadan

Oxford is a trade mark of Oxford University Press

ISBN 0 19 833178

Set by Tradespools Ltd, Frome, Somerset
Printed in Great Britain
by Thomson Litho Ltd, East Kilbride, Scotland

A CIP catalogue record for this book is available from the British Library.

CONTENTS

CONTENTS

CONTENTS

CONTENTS

CONTENTS

The Moment

To write down all I contain at this moment
I would pour the desert through an hour-glass,
The sea through a water-clock,
Grain by grain and drop by drop
Let in the trackless, measureless, mutable seas and sands.

For earth's days and nights are breaking over me
The tides and sands are running through me,
And I have only two hands and a heart to hold the desert and the sea.

What can I contain of it? It escapes and eludes me
The tides wash me away
The desert shifts under my feet.

Kathleen Raine

'The poem reminds us of what we ourselves know, but did not know we knew.'

Kathleen Raine

HOW TO USE THIS BOOK

The aim of this book is to deepen understanding, and enjoyment, of English poetry through writing – mainly writing poetry. It has two parts:

The Anthology

The poems need to be read and digested. Try especially to read them aloud. Very often they can be read by a group. Talking about how to read a poem is often the best way of coming to understand it. We will ask you questions about the poems. Most of these don't have right or wrong answers. They are to help you talk, to help you work out what you think. Your honest response to the poem is the most important thing.

Talk about each poem using our four ways into a poem:

Story

What is the poem about? Some poems tell a story, others describe a moment or a feeling.

Feeling

What feelings does the poem give you?

Pattern

How is the poem arranged on the page? Why do the lines end where they do? Does it have a regular rhythm? What about the sound of the words?

Image

What pictures does it create in your mind? How does it do this?
Many people think best when they doodle. Roger McGough describes on page 84 how a poem grew out of a cartoon. Small children are often asked to illustrate a poem. Don't dismiss it as a childish idea. Try doodling whatever comes into your head as you read.

Learning whole poems, or parts of them, by heart can help you to understand them. They then become part of you in a way in which they cannot be otherwise.

We have also included six sections in which we focus on individual poets to give you a flavour of each poet's writing, and an idea of his or her approach. The three living focused poets have written notes on their poems.

Throughout the book we use some technical terms. To avoid a lot of repetition we explain them just once. We have designed the book so that one page leads on to another, but you don't have to work all the way through from the beginning.

Suggestions for Writing

We assume that you will have read the poem and talked about it before you try to write.

People have three main worries about writing, especially writing poetry:

1 **Embarrassment.** Poetry is often seen as very personal. Readers usually think that the 'I' of a poem is the writer even though we know that the 'I' of a novel isn't. Jeni Couzyn, some of whose poems you can read on pages 50 and 51, says, 'There was never a teacher I could talk to about writing . . . poems one wrote oneself, which were private and sacred.' This is why we concentrate on skills and models. On these everyone in the class can meet on safe, neutral ground. What you write from the heart can then, if you wish, be kept private.

2 People **worry** too much about being **original**. Think about poetry writing as a skill you want to acquire, like handwriting. When you started learning to write you copied. Your own style came later. So with poetry: copy those who are good at it. We will often suggest that you imitate a poem or a poet's style because imitating a poem you like is a good way to learn. Your own style will develop in time. There are two main ways to imitate:

a **Pastiche:** this means to write like someone else because you admire them. It's a serious exercise.

b **Parody:** this is to write like someone to make a joke out of them.

3 People sit and wait for **inspiration** – and you could wait for years. The only way to learn to write is to write. Again, remember that you are practising a skill. It doesn't matter what you practise on. That is why we have included so many poems about pictures or other writing. You can take any picture and write a poem about it. We have also included many poems about school because it's all around you and goes back probably as far as you can remember.

The waiting-for-inspiration worry also makes people think that poems drop out of the sky all complete. John Betjeman, who became Poet Laureate, wrote in his verse autobiography:

I knew as soon as I could read and write
That I must be a poet . . .
And so, at sunset, off to Hampstead Heath
I went with pencil and with writing-pad
And stood tip-toe upon a little hill
Awaiting inspiration from the sky.
'Look! there's a poet!' people might exclaim
On footpaths near . . .

but he was never happy with what came from his inspiration.

HOW TO USE THIS BOOK

We have included several examples to show how poets have revised what they have written, sometimes even after the poem has been printed. Inspiration will often come after you have started writing and your ideas may surprise you. The important thing is just to write.

We have concentrated on suggestions for writing poems. You can, of course, write in other ways, responding to a poem with a story, a play or a letter. Exercises in this book which involve writing are marked with the symbol ✥.

Handwriting Poems

Think of writing in stages, a handful of stages that between them will catch the poem:

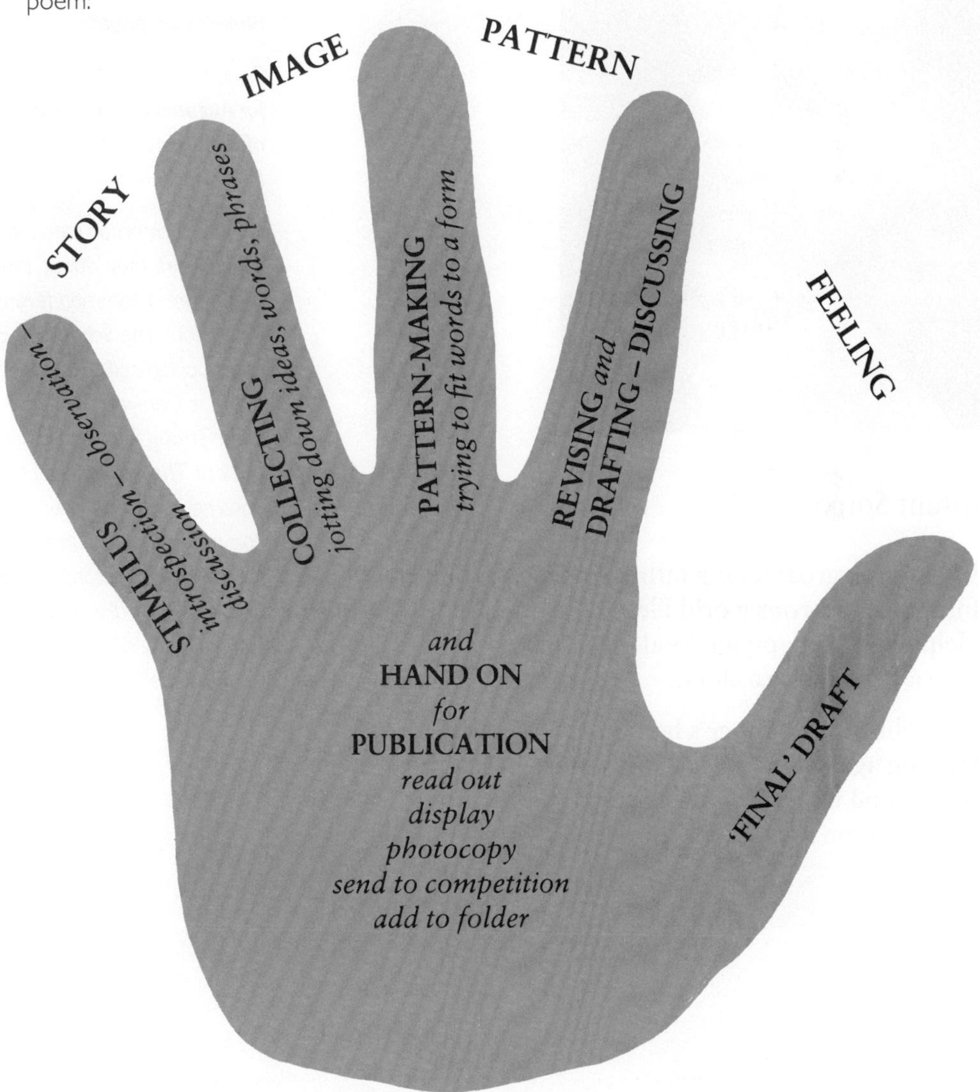

WILLIAM BLAKE

William Blake was born in 1757, the third son of a London stocking-maker. He didn't go to school. He was apprenticed to an engraver. Engraving was then the main way of producing multiple copies of a picture. In 1782 he married Catherine Boucher but they had no children. He engraved and published his **Songs of Innocence** in 1789 and, among many other books, **Songs of Experience** in 1794. His books were not popular in his own lifetime and he died poor in 1827.

Infant Sorrow

My mother groan'd, my father wept,
Into the dangerous world I leapt;
Helpless, naked, piping loud,
Like a fiend hid in a cloud.

Struggling in my father's hands,
Striving against my swaddling bands,
Bound and weary, I thought best
To sulk upon my mother's breast.

The illustrations in this section are copies of Blake's own pages.

Read through this section, all of which, except for **Auguries of Innocence**, *comes from* **Songs of Experience**. *As you read, try to answer these questions:*

Is there a common idea running through his poems? Are they 'about' the same things? Do they share a common feeling?
Talk about **The Schoolboy**. *Blake never went to school himself but he has strong feelings about it. Can you find other examples of the same strong feeling in other poems of his?*
Look at **The Schoolboy**. *How many questions does he ask in this poem? What does he compare schoolchildren to? How does he use the changing seasons? Does he use images from the natural world in his other poems?*
Can you now say what is special and typical about Blake's style?

WILLIAM BLAKE

The Schoolboy

I love to rise in a summer morn,
When the birds sing on every tree;
The distant huntsman winds his horn,
And the sky-lark sings with me.
O! what sweet company.

But to go to school in a summer morn,
O! it drives all joy away;
Under a cruel eye outworn,
The little ones spend the day
In sighing and dismay.

Ah! then at times I drooping sit,
And spend many an anxious hour,
Nor in my book can I take delight,
Nor sit in learning's bower,
Worn thro' with the dreary shower.

How can the bird that is born for joy,
Sit in a cage and sing?
How can a child, when fears annoy,
But droop his tender wing,
And forget his youthful spring?

O! father and mother, if buds are nipp'd,
And blossoms blown away,
And if the tender plants are stripp'd
Of their joy in the springing day,
By sorrow and care's dismay,

How shall the summer arise in joy
Or the summer fruits appear?
Or how shall we gather what griefs destroy
Or bless the mellowing year,
When the blasts of winter appear?

WILLIAM BLAKE

A Poison Tree

I was angry with my friend:
I told my wrath, my wrath did end.
I was angry with my foe:
I told it not, my wrath did grow.

And I water'd it in fears,
Night and morning with my tears;
And I sunned it with smiles,
And with soft deceitful wiles.

And it grew both day and night,
Till it bore an apple bright;
And my foe beheld it shine,
And he knew that it was mine,

And into my garden stole,
When the night had veil'd the pole;
In the morning glad I see
My foe outstretch'd beneath the tree.

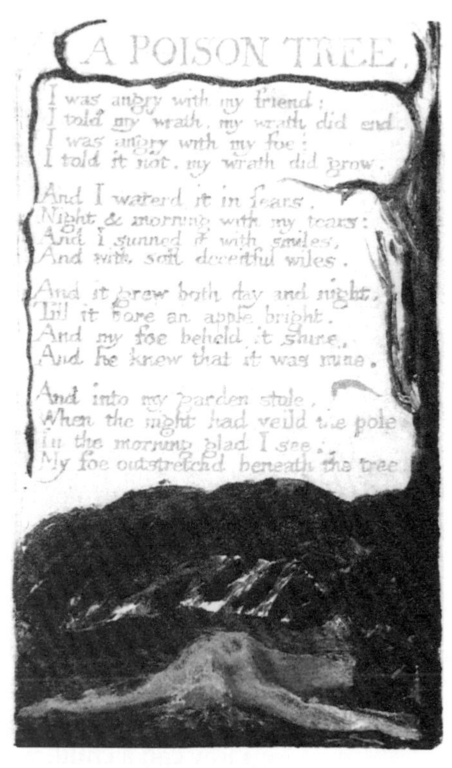

The Sick Rose

O Rose, thou art sick!
The invisible worm,
That flies in the night
In the howling storm,

Has found out thy bed
Of crimson joy;
And his dark secret love
Does thy life destroy.

The Lily

The modest Rose puts forth a thorn,
The humble Sheep, a threat'ning horn;
While the Lily white shall in Love delight,
Nor a thorn nor a threat stain her beauty bright.

WILLIAM BLAKE

from Auguries of Innocence

To see a World in a grain of sand,
And a Heaven in a wild flower,
Hold Infinity in the palm of your hand,
And Eternity in an hour.

A robin redbreast in a cage
Puts all Heaven in a rage.

A dove-house fill'd with doves and pigeons
Shudders Hell thro' all its regions.

A dog starv'd at his master's gate
Predicts the ruin of the State.

A horse misus'd upon the road
Calls to Heaven for human blood.

Each outcry of the hunted hare
A fibre from the brain does tear.

A skylark wounded in the wing,
A cherubim does cease to sing.

The lamb misus'd breeds public strife,
And yet forgives the butcher's knife.

The bat that flits at close of eve
Has left the brain that won't believe.

The owl that calls upon the night
Speaks the unbeliever's fright.

The wanton boy that kills the fly
Shall feel the spider's enmity.

A truth that's told with bad intent
Beats all the lies you can invent.
It is right it should be so;
Man was made for joy and woe;
And when this we rightly know,
Thro' the world we safely go.
Joy and woe are woven fine,
A clothing for the soul divine;

Under every grief and pine
Runs a joy with silken twine.

WILLIAM BLAKE

The Tiger

Tiger! Tiger! burning bright
In the forests of the night,
What immortal hand or eye
Could frame thy fearful symmetry?

In what distant deeps or skies
Burnt the fire of thine eyes?
On what wings dare he aspire?
What the hand dare seize the fire?

And what shoulder, and what art
Could twist the sinews of thy heart?
And, when thy heart began to beat,
What dread hand? and what dread feet?

What the hammer? what the chain?
In what furnace was thy brain?
What the anvil? what dread grasp
Dare its deadly terrors clasp?

When the stars threw down their spears,
And water'd heaven with their tears,
Did he smile his work to see?
Did he who made the lamb make thee?

Tiger! Tiger! burning bright
In the forests of the night,
What immortal hand or eye
Dare frame thy fearful symmetry?

This is Blake's most famous poem, but one which is not very easy to understand. Fortunately we have Blake's drafts, and if we study them we may understand the poem better. They were written on facing pages of a notebook, and we have reprinted them opposite. In the left-hand column here is what Blake wrote on the left-hand page, with the right-hand page in the right-hand column. The italics show where words were crossed out. There was no punctuation.

There is another version of line 12:

> What dread hand forged thy
> dread feet?

This is certainly clearer, but do you like it better?

✜ *Make up your own version of the poem by choosing whichever lines you like from the drafts, and read the poem out loud. Whose version is most popular?*

On one level Blake is writing about the wonder of the tiger, and so of creation itself. On another level, perhaps, the tiger represents evil in the world. ('The lamb' is sometimes used as another name for Christ.)

How can you read Blake's final version to bring out the strength and danger of the tiger?

WILLIAM BLAKE

The Tyger

1 Tyger Tyger burning bright
In the forests of the night
What immortal hand & eye
or
Could frame thy fearful symmetry
Dare

2 *In what* distant deeps or skies
Burnt in
Burnt the fire of thine eyes
The cruel
On what wings dare he aspire
What the hand dare sieze the fire

3 And what shoulder & what art
Could twist the sinews of thy heart
And when thy heart began to beat
What dread hand & what dread feet
Could fetch it from the furnace deep
And in thy horrid ribs dare steep
In the well of sanguine woe
In what clay & in what mould
Were thy eyes of fury rolld

4 *What* the hammer *what* the chain
Where *where*
In what furnace was thy brain
What the anvil What *the arm*
arm
grasp
clasp
dread grasp
Could its deadly terrors *clasp*
Dare *grasp*
clasp

6 Tyger Tyger burning bright
In the forests of the night
What immortal hand & eye
Dare *form* thy fearful symmetry
frame

[*On the opposite page*]

Burnt in distant deeps or skies
The cruel fire of thine eyes
Could heart descend or wings aspire
What the hand dare siese the fire

5 3 And *did he laugh* his work to see
dare he *smile*
laugh
What the shoulder *what the knee*
ankle
4 *Did* he who made the lamb make thee
Dare
1 When the stars threw down their spears
2 And waterd heaven with their tears

You may think that Blake is a poet of protest. What would he protest about if he were writing today?

✤ *Write more couplets for* **Auguries of Innocence***, perhaps about the killing of whales, factory farming, zoos.*

✤ *Choose another animal and write about it in a poem like* **The Tiger***. You could write a parody about a hamster or goldfish, or a pastiche about whatever animal you really admire. You could write about people in the same way.*

There is a pastiche of Blake on page 19 and a parody on page 76.

'The difference between a bad artist and a good one is: The bad artist seems to copy a great deal; the good one really does.'

William Blake

The Tyger.

Tyger Tyger, burning bright,
In the forests of the night;
What immortal hand or eye,
Could frame thy fearful symmetry?

In what distant deeps or skies.
Burnt the fire of thine eyes?
On what wings dare he aspire?
What the hand, dare sieze the fire?

And what shoulder, & what art.
Could twist the sinews of thy heart?
And when thy heart began to beat,
What dread hand? & what dread feet?

What the hammer? what the chain,
In what furnace was thy brain?
What the anvil? what dread grasp.
Dare its deadly terrors clasp!

When the stars threw down their spears
And water'd heaven with their tears:
Did he smile his work to see?
Did he who made the Lamb make thee?

Tyger Tyger burning bright,
In the forests of the night:
What immortal hand or eye,
Dare frame thy fearful symmetry?

A Man may be Happy

I feel that a man may be happy in This World.
And I know that This World
Is a World of imagination & Vision.
I see All I Paint In This World,
But Every body does not see alike.
To the eyes of a Miser a Guinea
Is more beautiful than the Sun,
& a bag worn with the use of Money
Has more beautiful proportions
Than a Vine filled with Grapes.
The tree which moves some to tears of joy
Is in the eyes of others
Only a green thing that stands in the way.

Adrian Mitchell

This was written as a song for a play about William Blake. It is an example of pastiche.

✤ *Continue this poem with other contrasting ways of looking at things. Your poem could be about some of the following things: rain/snow/wind/telephone/bus/dog/school. Start:*

> ***But everybody does not see alike.***
> ***To the eyes of . . .***

Adrian Mitchell always requests that none of his work should be used in connection with any exam whatsoever. He believes 'The examination system is an educational experiment which has failed. It has been partly responsible for the unprecedented unpopularity of poetry in Britain. Poems should be read, recited, sung and danced on a purely voluntary basis. They should not be made the subject of endless boring and repetitive essays by people who don't like the poems in the first place, and they should not be dissected like so many dead frogs. While exams persist, poetry should be what happens behind the bike sheds.'

> *'There are usually two stages in making a poem. The hot scribble stage. And the cold carving stage.'*
> *Adrian Mitchell*

Nursery Rhymes

Mother, you didn't tell me

that the Witch lived on the bomb-site down the road, where
the House That Jack Built foundered, rubble-dust and weed;
her familiars were the prehistoric earthmovers with their
insect jaws, and cranes like skeletons of knights in
armour swinging slow murderous iron balls . . .

that the Three Bears grumbled and roared at each other in
the house next door; their Goldilocks, frail changeling
daughter, played in the yard, a hundred miles away; she
never spoke to me . . .

that the Man in the Moon was my Uncle Tom; he stared at his
reflection in an endless sea like the face of a drowned twin;
'Out, get out,' he raged at Wynken, Blynken, Nod and me;
we perturbed his immaculate loneliness . . .

that Grandmother ate the Wolf; 'No Hawkers No Pedlars', and
she meant it, with an axe-glint in her eye; one night,
small howls, struggles, a hush behind her bedroom door;
next morning 'Grandma's gone away . . .'; the Wolf was free . . .

No, mother, you didn't tell me the half of it.
Maybe you had forgotten. But I knew,

I always knew.

Philip Gross

Household Dilemma

'If I may make a point'
she said
'It is this.
When I come home, tired,
from a hard day's work,
I do not wish
to be greeted
by a sinkful
of dirty
WASHING-UP'.
And she banged their heads
together
for their understanding.
'Vinegar and brown paper
and fie to you too'
cried the children.
And they went to bed sulky.
But the little plates
in the sink
and the big spoon
and the baked beany pan
chortled
and cuddled their grease.

Angie Gilligan

These are examples of poems that use other writing as a starting point. Childish things (nursery rhymes and fairy tales) are used here to make comments about childhood.

What nursery rhymes are used in the two poems?
How have they been used differently in the two poems?
Do they make the poems seem childish?

✤ *Rewrite a sugary fairy tale to make it more realistic. For example, Prince Charming goes to find the one woman the glass slipper fits. How many people in the class have the same shoe size? How many women in the land would have had the same shoe size as Cinderella? Write a poem about all the women who take the same size shoe fighting over the glass slipper. Give it a message, perhaps about lack of planning, or greed.*

The Prodigal Son

He is far off, he is very far off, he's a blur
Of shadow against the setting sun, he is ragged
Clearly and slow and there is a touch of shame
And even penitence. In his vineyards his father
Is gazing at the crop, the promising early
Fruits but suddenly for no apparent reason
He lifts his torso, tilts his head and shades
His eye and something very familiar, a gesture
Of a child who has misbehaved is silhouetted
Against the bonfire blaze, 'It is my son at last, at last it is
My dear lost son, my promising one, the part
Of my heart I've missed for nearly a dozen years.'

In the kitchen a clatter of dishes proceeds and good
Herby smells rise up but the father is running
Fleet as a boy again and the shadow too turns
In an old and hopeless way. The boy doesn't move
For he is still a boy to his father. The sky
Is festive pink and purple. The father throws arms
About the boy and kisses the thin pinched face,
Smells the dirty clothes and a godlike but also extremely
Human compassion is seen against the light
And the boy is crying babyishly but now
Treading slowly the old good road to home
Through olive trees and herbs and the starting grapes

But in the house someone is slamming doors
And swearing and saying 'It isn't fair. I was good'
And the prodigal is afraid till his father goes
And coaxes the elder son to the gala meal,
And grapes it seems have been burst across the sky.
Wine is running along the slopes of night
As a household starts to heal.

Elizabeth Jennings

These are two poems about people who run away from home. The first was inspired by a story in the Bible (St Luke's Gospel, chapter 15, verses 11 to 32).

✤ *Make a list of all the times vines are used as an image throughout the poem.*

✤ *Take another parable and turn it into a poem. Can you think of a suitable image to use through your poem? You could base your poem on one of the following.*

The Sower: Mark 4, 1–8.
The Labourers in the Vineyard: Mark 20, 1–16
The Great Supper: Luke 14, 15–24
The Talents: Matthew 25, 14–30

The Ice Factory

('Not a great deal is known about this minor industry,
which appears to have had a short life . . .'
Helen Harris, The Industrial Archaeology of Dartmoor)

A hush like a shut Bible. Father: 'Grace
will wait . . .' The latch clacks. Our stare
lifts from our cold meat, from the empty place
to the door, and cousin Joseph. His chair
grates on the flags, and Father: '*Now*
let us pray . . .'.
Who knew him? Slow
to speak or laugh, slow at the plough,
some kind of fool, they said. I'd go
to fetch him in from the topmost field:
'This place don't give us nothing free
but rain. So Father says.' He smiled.

November: bitter drizzle. He
went up the hillside as the cloud came down.
December: snow penned us behind doors.
The first clear morning, we'd see thin
tracks, wavering slightly, up into the moor.
In March, I followed. Jumbled stone
in a windy hollow; black peat-water riffling;
a turf-wadded hut. 'You've come alone?'
He prised the door, 'Then look.' Nothing,
I saw nothing, or a glistening black, before
the ice-cold took my breath. His chill
smile: 'Things aren't always where
they're needed. Are we, girl?'
April,
he was gone. Was seen, halfway to town,
cart lumbering under bales of moss and straw,
steaming and dripping. 'Taking water down,'
they laughed, 'Thought that's what river's for.'

Then nothing. Though the horse was found
by the docks where the tall ships come. All year
they traded stories – 'mad', 'enlisted', 'drowned'
– and tell them still for any stranger's beer
since the farm's gone back to moor. And now
this flimsy envelope: '. . . New York'. Inside,
'My father would have wished . . .'
He was rich somehow;
had grandsons; mentioned me before he died.

Philip Gross

*In **The Ice Factory**, notice how the lines run on. How many lines end with the end of a sentence? Does it make the poem difficult to read aloud? Does it make you notice the rhymes less? Why do you think this rather vague pattern is used?*

✣ *Write a story telling what happened from Joseph's point-of-view.*

Beyond Words

That row of icicles along the gutter
Feels like my armoury of hate;
And you, you . . . you, you utter . . .
You wait.

Robert Frost

How does the first poem use words and punctuation and repetition to show someone almost speechless with rage?

What image does it have? Does it fit the feeling the writer has?

Spite Shots Labels

Wouldn't it be good
if as they grow
bodies could show
rammed-in pins and nails exposed –
spite bullets, all tagged –
at head, hand, tummy, bum,
showing where they came from,
why launched
and when due to be returned.

James Berry

The second poem seems calmer. How does the writer share his feelings with the reader? Which words create a feeling of menace?

✜ *Try using words to create feelings of boredom/waiting/fear, etc.*

Little Johnny's Final Letter

Mother,
I won't be home this evening, so
don't worry; don't hurry to report me missing.
Don't drain the canals to find me,
I've decided to stay alive, don't
search the woods, I'm not hiding,
simply gone to get myself classified.
Don't leave my shreddies out,
I've done with security.
Don't circulate my photograph to society
I have disguised myself as a man
and am giving priority to obscurity.
It suits me fine;
I have taken off my short trousers
and put on long ones, and
now am going out into the city, so
don't worry; don't hurry to report me missing.

I've rented a room without any curtains
and sit behind the windows growing cold,
heard your plea on the radio this morning,
you sounded sad and strangely old...

Brian Patten

What is the feeling in this poem? Does that feeling change when the pattern changes in the last stanza?

Make a list of the ways in which the pattern of this poem differs from a real letter.

✤ *Write a poem-letter: a thank-you for a Christmas present; an excuse for missing school; an application for a job; a letter to the Prime Minister. Make your poem different from a real letter in the ways you noted in your list.*

Like a Beacon

In London
every now and then
I get this craving
for my mother's food
I leave art galleries
in search of plantains
saltfish/sweet potatoes

I need this link

I need this touch
of home
swinging my bag
like a beacon
against the cold

Grace Nichols

What is the writer feeling?
What do you miss most when you are away from home?

✤ *Start a poem:*
I need this touch
of home ...
You could have one verse for each sense: sight, smell, taste, sound, touch.

'A poet can discover things in her own poetry ... You don't know quite where the poem will take you because it has a living mind or spirit of its own.'
Grace Nichols

Fern Hill

Now as I was young and easy under the apple boughs
About the lilting house and happy as the grass was green,
    The night above the dingle starry,
        Time let me hail and climb
    Golden in the heydays of his eyes,
And honoured among wagons I was prince of the apple towns
And once below a time I lordly had the trees and leaves
        Trail with daisies and barley
    Down the rivers of the windfall light.

And as I was green and carefree, famous among the barns
About the happy yard and singing as the farm was home,
    In the sun that is young once only,
        Time let me play and be
    Golden in the mercy of his means,
And green and golden I was huntsman and herdsman, the calves
Sang to my horn, the foxes on the hills barked clear and cold,
        And the sabbath rang slowly
    In the pebbles of the holy streams.

All the sun long it was running, it was lovely, the hay
Fields high as the house, the tunes from the chimneys, it was air
    And playing, lovely and watery
        And fire green as grass.
    And nightly under the simple stars
As I rode to sleep the owls were bearing the farm away,
All the moon long I heard, blessed among stables, the nightjars
    Flying with the ricks, and the horses
        Flashing into the dark.

And then to awake, and the farm, like a wanderer white
With the dew, come back, the cock on his shoulder: it was all
    Shining, it was Adam and maiden,
        The sky gathered again
    And the sun grew round that very day.
So it must have been after the birth of the simple light
In the first, spinning place, the spellbound horses walking warm
    Out of the whinnying green stable
        On to the fields of praise.

And honoured among foxes and pheasants by the gay house
Under the new made clouds and happy as the heart was long,
   In the sun born over and over,
      I ran my heedless ways,
   My wishes raced through the house high hay
And nothing I cared, at my sky blue trades, that time allows
In all his tuneful turning so few and such morning songs
   Before the children green and golden
      Follow him out of grace,

Nothing I cared, in the lamb white days, that time would take me
Up to the swallow thronged loft by the shadow of my hand,
   In the moon that is always rising,
      Nor that riding to sleep
   I should hear him fly with the high fields
And wake to the farm forever fled from the childless land.
Oh as I was young and easy in the mercy of his means,
      Time held me green and dying
      Though I sang in my chains like the sea.

Dylan Thomas

Once *below* a time
all the *sun* long
happy as the *heart* was long

Why could these be called examples of word-play? Find other examples.
Look for the phrases where unexpected adjectives are used: lilting house; windfall light; holy streams. How many can you find?
Look for the echoes of the story of Adam and Eve (Genesis, chapter 3).
How many references to time can you find?
What is the rhythm of the lines?

All these elements are typical of Dylan Thomas.

✣ *As a warm-up exercise write some descriptions using unexpected adjectives. Make them as fantastic as you can.*

✣ *Take one particular incident or moment when you were younger, and use it as the basis for a poem. Try especially to use unusual adjectives and word-play in the way that Dylan Thomas does. Keep rereading* **Fern Hill** *and your poem should become a pastiche.*

'Poetry is what in a poem makes you laugh, cry, prickle, be silent, makes your toenails twinkle . . .'
Dylan Thomas

RHYTHM

The **pattern** of a poem is shaped by the combined **rhythm** of its words and lines. Often, this pattern and rhythm will give you an additional sense of satisfaction when you hear or read the words, in the same way that rhythm in music gives pattern to the sounds and an additional dimension to those sounds.

All rhythm, whether musical or verbal, consists of beats or stresses. Any English word of more than one syllable has one stressed syllable, with the rest unstressed. Consider, and say to yourself, the following examples: wonderful, purpose, imagine, progress (*noun*), progress (*verb*).

Poetry often has a number of stresses to each line, and these lines have formal names according to the number of stresses:

2 stresses per line: ***Dimeter***

> O Rose, thou art sick!
> The invisible worm

3 stresses: ***Trimeter***

> O have you caught the tiger?
> And can you hold him tight?

4 stresses: ***Tetrameter***

> My father made the walls resound

5 stresses: ***Pentameter***

> Well do I call to mind the very week
> When I was first entrusted to the care

6 stresses: ***Hexameter***

> Now as I was young and easy under the apple boughs

7 stresses: ***Heptameter***

> I must down to the seas again, to the lonely sea and the sky

As you read lines of poetry, try to be aware of the rhythm and the number of stresses to a line.

Autobiography

In my childhood trees were green
And there was plenty to be seen.

Come back early or never come.

My father made the walls resound,
He wore his collar the wrong way round.

Come back early or never come.

My mother wore a yellow dress;
Gently, gently, gentleness.

Come back early or never come.

When I was five the black dreams came;
Nothing after was quite the same.

Come back early or never come.

The dark was talking to the dead;
The lamp was dark beside my bed.

Come back early or never come.

When I woke they did not care;
Nobody, nobody was there.

Come back early or never come.

When my silent terror cried,
Nobody, nobody replied.

Come back early or never come.

I got up; the chilly sun
Saw me walk away alone.

Come back early or never come.

Louis MacNeice

✤ *This poem gives a pattern to copy:*

In my childhood . . .
chorus
My father . . .
chorus
My mother . . .
chorus
When I was five . . .

and then continue as you like.

Translators take a poem written in, say, French and change it into English. However, we can translate poems in a different way, changing not just the language in which a poem is written, but also the images which it uses. Here, St Francis' **Hymn to the Sun** *has been translated from the original Italian into English haiku and into Hollywood 'gangsterese'.*

Many poems are about the countryside; many were written in the past. The images they use are not those of our everyday life. Poetry seems sometimes to be all daffodils and sheep, and the language is old-fashioned too.

We can take poems that use old-fashioned images and translate those images into modern images, images from electronics, physics, supermarkets, mass media, nuclear arms.

The Canticle of the Sun

Be glad for Brother
Sun who brings the shining day
And lends us his warmth.

Be glad for Sister
Moon and the stars. Their cold lights
Take fear from the dark.

Be glad for Brother
Wind, for clear skies, clouds that make
Each day dawn new-made.

Be glad for Sister
Water who washes us clean
And refreshes us.

Be glad for Brother
Fire who flickers in flames to
Warm our winter cold.

Be glad for Mother
Earth who gives us life: fruit, flowers,
In her harvest time.

adapted from the words of
Saint Francis of Assisi

Michael Richards

St Francis's 'Cantico di Frate Sole' done into Hollywood gangsterese

Boss, you got it all –
admiration, pull, status, the works –
it's all yours.

It's yours for being top –
there ain't no guy not too green
to mention you.

Thanks, for you and your organisation,
specially this guy Sun
who's always around with some light;

there's class stamped all over him,
a real smart guy –
he could only be one of your boys Boss.

Thanks, Boss, for these dames Moon and Stars,
platinum blondes in the night
you made real sweet.

Thanks, Boss, for this guy Wind
and the Weather boys, Air, Cloud, Sky,
bringing your gang the goods.

Thanks, Boss, for this dame Water –
she's a cute kid
and don't try to come over too big.

Thanks, Boss, for this guy Fire
who keeps his eye open after dark,
don't squeal and can handle himself.

Thanks, Boss, for old Ma Earth –
she looks after us real good,
always flowers and stuff around the joint.

Thanks, Boss, for the guys who take the rap
when you tell 'em,
that get roughed up and see trouble;

the smart guys know to keep their mouths shut
'cause you'll see to it Boss
they're on the payroll.

Thanks, Boss, for this cold dame Death
no guy can escape.
Nuts to the guys that die playing dirty.

Smart guys die in your good books.
There ain't no second show-down.

O.K. you guys, get prayin' –
say thanks to the Boss
and don't get big ideas.

Steve Ellis

Follower

My father worked with a horse-plough.
His shoulders globed like a full sail strung
Between the shafts and the furrow.
The horses strained at his clicking tongue.

An expert. He would set the wing
And fit the bright steel-pointed sock.
The sod rolled over without breaking.
At the headrig, with a single pluck

Of reins, the sweating team turned round
And back into the land. His eye
Narrowed and angled at the ground,
Mapping the furrow exactly.

I stumbled in his hob-nailed wake,
Fell sometimes on the polished sod;
Sometimes he rode me on his back
Dipping and rising to his plod.

I wanted to grow up and plough,
To close one eye, stiffen my arm.
All I ever did was follow
In his broad shadow round the farm.

I was a nuisance, tripping, falling,
Yapping always. But today
It is my father who keeps stumbling
Behind me, and will not go away.

Seamus Heaney

This poem gives you something to translate. It is written about a childhood in old-fashioned countryside. How could you get the same ideas into modern times, and a town setting?

Charlotte, her Book

I am Charlotte. I don't say hello
to people and sometimes I bite.
Although I am dead I still jump
out of bed and wake them up at night.

This is my mother. Her hair is blue
and I have drawn her with no eyes
and arms like twigs. I don't do
what I'm told and I tell lies.

This is my father. He has a mouth
under his left ear. I'm fed up
with drawing people, so I scribble
smoke and cover his head right up.

I am a brat kid, fostered out because
my mother is sick in the head,
and I would eat her if I could,
and make her good and dead.

Although I am only four I went away
so soon they hardly knew me,
and stars sprang out of my eyes,
and cold winds blew me.

My mother always says she loves me.
My father says he loves me too.
I love Charlotte. A car ran
over Charlotte. This is her book.

Elizabeth Bartlett

Who is Charlotte? What facts do we learn about her? What are her feelings?

This is a harsh poem. Where does its harshness come from? Notice the references to a child's drawing in the poem. We normally think of children's drawings as 'sweet', but is that the case here?

✤ *Look for a child's picture. What conventional feeling does it represent? Write a poem that goes with it, but whose feelings are quite different.*

The Almond Tree

I
All the way to the hospital
the lights were green as peppermints.
Trees of black iron broke into leaf
ahead of me, as if
I were the lucky prince
in an enchanted wood
summoning summer with my whistle,
banishing winter with a nod.

Swung by the road from bend to bend,
I was aware that blood was running
down through the delta of my wrist
and under arches
of bright bone. Centuries,
continents it had crossed;
from an undisclosed beginning
spiralling to an unmapped end.

II
Crossing (at sixty) Magdalen Bridge
Let it be a son, a son, said
the man in the driving mirror,
Let it be a son. The tower
held up its hand: the college
bells shook their blessing on his head.

III
I parked in an almond's
shadow blossom, for the tree
was waving, waving me
upstairs with a child's hands.

IV
Up
the spinal stair
and at the top
along
a bone-white corridor
the blood tide swung
me swung me to a room
whose walls shuddered
with the shuddering womb.
Under the sheet
wave after wave, wave
after wave beat
on the bone coast, bringing
ashore – whom?
New-
minted, my bright farthing!
Coined by our love, stamped with
our images, how you
enrich us! Both
you make one. Welcome
to your white sheet,
my best poem!

V
At seven-thirty
the visitors' bell
scissored the calm
of the corridors.
The doctor walked with me
to the slicing doors.
His hand upon my arm,
his voice – *I have to tell
you* – set another bell
beating in my head:
your son is a mongol
the doctor said.

VI
How easily the word went in –
clean as a bullet
leaving no mark on the skin,
stopping the heart within it.

This was my first death.
The '*I*' ascending on a slow
last thermal breath
studied the man below

* * *

VII
The hospital – its heavy freight
lashed down ship-shape ward over ward –
steamed into night with some on board
soon to be lost if the desperate

charts were known. Others would come
altered to land or find the land
altered. At their voyage's end
some would be added to, some

diminished. In a numbered cot
my son sailed from me; never to come
ashore into my kingdom
speaking my language. Better not

look that way. The almond tree . . .

* * *

In the days we have known one another,
my little mongol love,
I have learnt more from your lips
than you will from mine perhaps:
I have learnt that to live is to suffer,
to suffer is to live.

Jon Stallworthy

This poem has been shortened.

Here the writer thinks about his first-born child, a son who was born with what is now called Down's Syndrome.

Look at each part of the poem in turn. What images are used in each part?

The feelings in this poem see-saw about.

✣ *Think of a time or an incident in your life when you have had strong and changing feelings (you can, if you prefer, choose to write about a fictional 'you'). What sort of poem could you write about it? What images would you choose?*

> *'Poets usually begin to write poems because they have read other people's and like them so much they want to write one themselves.'*
> *Jon Stallworthy*

IMAGE

Words can be used to create pictures in your mind, to help you **see** something:

> as green as peppermints
> clean as a bullet

When we say that something is like something else, that is a **simile**. A simile is introduced by **like** or **as**.

When we compare two separate things but leave out the **like** or **as**, that is a **metaphor**:

> trees of black iron
> the tower held up its hand
> up the spinal staircase
> a bone-white corridor
> scissored the calm

Sometimes a metaphor talks of a thing as if it were a person: that is called **personification**:

> the tree was waving

Sometimes a poem will use the same metaphor for all or most of the poem; we call this **extended metaphor**. An example of extended metaphor is **Wall** on page 47.

Our everyday language is full of similes and metaphors that are 'dead' because they are so common that they no longer create fresh pictures in our minds. **A blanket of snow** may originally have been a startling image, but now it has been used too often to be anything except a cliché.

Remember that **images** do not have to be visual: other senses can be used.

In **The Almond Tree**, for example, notice how the author introduces touch

> swung by the road

and hearing

> the college bells shook their blessing.

WILLIAM WORDSWORTH

William Wordsworth was born at Cockermouth in the Lake District in 1770. With his friend Samuel Taylor Coleridge he was one of the early leaders of English Romanticism. In the preface to **Lyrical Ballads**, which he published with Coleridge, he proposed a reform in the sort of vocabulary used in poetry which would encourage 'a selection of language really used by men'. (This obviously meant language used in his day – some of the words in his poetry seem old-fashioned to us.)

He was appointed Poet Laureate in 1843 and died in 1850; he was buried at Grasmere, in the Lake District, an area with which he will always be associated.

In his writing he described his work as 'emotion recollected in tranquility'; and we shall see from several of the following examples of his work that there is often a considerable time lapse between his 'inspiration' and his composition.

And in the Frosty Season

And in the frosty season, when the sun
Was set, and visible for many a mile
The cottage windows through the twilight blaz'd,
I heeded not the summons: – happy time
It was, indeed, for all of us; to me
It was a time of rapture: clear and loud
The village clock toll'd six; I wheel'd about,
Proud and exulting, like an untired horse,
That cares not for his home. – All shod with steel,
We hiss'd along the polish'd ice, in games
Confederate, imitative of the chase
And woodland pleasures, the resounding horn,
The Pack loud bellowing, and the hunted hare.
So through the darkness and the cold we flew,
And not a voice was idle; with the din,
Meanwhile, the precipices rang aloud,
The leafless trees, and every icy crag
Tinkled like iron, while the distant hills
Into the tumult sent an alien sound
Of melancholy, not unnoticed, while the stars,
Eastward, were sparkling clear, and in the west
The orange sky of evening died away.

Prelude I

***The Prelude**, for which Wordsworth is perhaps best known, is a long, autobiographical poem. He gave it the subtitle **The Growth of a Poet's Mind**. Childhood memories naturally form much of the early part, and extracts from this part are included here. As you read these extracts, notice the regular rhythm of the lines – there are five beats/stresses to each line.*

WILLIAM WORDSWORTH

There Was a Boy

There was a Boy, ye knew him well, ye Cliffs
And Islands of Winander! many a time
At evening, when the stars had just begun
To move along the edges of the hills,
Rising or setting, would he stand alone
Beneath the trees, or by the glimmering Lake,
And there, with fingers interwoven, both hands
Press'd closely, palm to palm, and to his mouth
Uplifted, he, as through an instrument,
Blew mimic hootings to the silent owls
That they might answer him. – And they would shout
Across the watery Vale, and shout again,
Responsive to his call, with quivering peals,
And long halloos, and screams, and echoes loud
Redoubled and redoubled; concourse wild
Of mirth and jocund din! And when it chanced
That pauses of deep silence mock'd his skill,
Then sometimes, in that silence, while he hung
Listening, a gentle shock of mild surprize
Has carried far into his heart the voice
Of mountain torrents; or the visible scene
Would enter unawares into his mind
With all its solemn imagery, its rocks,
Its woods, and that uncertain Heaven, received
Into the bosom of the steady Lake.

Prelude V

In early drafts of ***There Was a Boy****, Wordsworth wrote in the first person, but changed to the third person for its publication in 1800. In a letter to Sir George Beaumont, on May 1st 1805, he wrote, 'It is a thing unprecedented in literary history that a man should talk so much about himself.'*

✣ *Change these extracts back into the first person; does it make any difference to the rhythm?*

'Poetry is the spontaneous overflow of powerful feelings.'
William Wordsworth

WILLIAM WORDSWORTH

Well do I Call to Mind

Well do I call to mind the very week
When I was first entrusted to the care
Of that sweet Valley; when its paths, its shores,
And brooks, were like a dream of novelty
To my half-infant thoughts; that very week
While I was roving up and down alone,
Seeking I knew not what, I chanced to cross
One of those open fields, which, shaped like ears,
Make green peninsulas on Esthwaite's Lake:
Twilight was coming on; yet through the gloom,
I saw distinctly on the opposite Shore
A heap of garments, left, as I supposed,
By one who there was bathing; long I watched,
But no one owned them; meanwhile the calm Lake
Grew dark, with all the shadows on its breast,
And, now and then, a fish up-leaping, snapped
The breathless stillness. The succeeding day,
(Those unclaimed garments telling a plain Tale)
Went there a Company, and, in their Boat
Sounded with grappling irons, and long poles.
At length, the dead Man, 'mid that beauteous scene
Of trees, and hills and water, bolt upright
Rose with his ghastly face; a spectre shape
Of terror even! and yet no vulgar fear,
Young as I was, a Child not nine years old,
Possessed me, for my inner eye had seen
Such sights before, among the shining streams
Of Fairy Land, the Forests of Romance:
Thence came a spirit hallowing what I saw
With decoration and ideal grace;
A dignity, a smoothness, like the works
Of Grecian Art, and purest Poesy.

Prelude V

The drowned man mentioned in this extract from ***The Prelude*** *was a local schoolmaster, James Jackson, who died on 18th June, 1779, when Wordsworth was nine years old.*

The style in which ***The Prelude*** *is written is called* ***blank verse****: 'blank' because there are no rhymes; 'verse' because the rhythm and length of lines are regular. Blank verse is usually written in iambic pentameters – an iambic pentameter has five beats in each line (see page 28 on Rhythm).*

'Poetry is the breath and finer spirit of all knowledge; it is the impassioned expression which is in the countenance of all Science.'

William Wordsworth

WILLIAM WORDSWORTH

Wordsworth was particularly fond of his younger sister, Dorothy, and lived with her in the Lake District for some years. They went walking together on long trips; and the following extract from her journal tells us of the sight that inspired Wordsworth's most famous poem, **The Daffodils**.

Wordsworth and Dorothy saw the daffodils on 15th April 1802, but the poem was composed between March 1804 and April 1807 and published in 1807; certainly an example of 'recollection of emotion in tranquility'.

[April] 15th, Thursday. It was a threatening, misty morning, but mild. We set off after dinner from Eusemere. Mrs Clarkson went a short way with us, but turned back. The wind was furious and we thought we must have returned. We first rested in the large boat-house, then under a furze bush opposite Mr Clarkson's. Saw the plough going into the field. The wind seized our breath. The Lake was rough. There was a boat by itself floating in the middle of the bay below Water Millock. We rested again in the Water Millock Lane. The hawthorns are black and green, the birches here and there greenish, but there is yet more of purple to be seen on the twigs. We got over into a field to avoid some cows – people working. A few primroses by the roadside – woodsorrel flower, the anemone, scentless violets, strawberries, and that starry yellow flower which Mrs C. calls pile wort. When we were in the woods beyond Gowbarrow Park we saw a few daffodils close to the water-side. We fancied that the lake had floated the seeds ashore, and that the little colony had so sprung up. But as we went along there were more and yet more; and at last, under the boughs of the trees, we saw that there was a long belt of them along the shore, about the breadth of a country turnpike road. I never saw daffodils so beautiful. They grew among the mossy stones about and about them; some rested their heads upon these stones as on a pillow for weariness; and the rest tossed and reeled and danced, and seemed as if they verily laughed with the wind, that blew upon them over the lake; they looked so gay, ever glancing, ever changing. This wind blew directly over the lake to them. There was here and there a little knot, and a few stragglers a few yards higher up; but they were so few as not to disturb the simplicity, unity, and life of that one busy highway.

N.B. Deer in Gowbarrow Park like skeletons.

Dorothy Wordsworth

WILLIAM WORDSWORTH

The Daffodils

I wandered lonely as a cloud
That floats on high o'er vales and hills,
When all at once I saw a crowd,
A host, of golden daffodils;
Beside the lake, beneath the trees,
Fluttering and dancing in the breeze.

Continuous as the stars that shine
And twinkle on the milky way,
They stretched in never-ending line
Along the margin of a bay:
Ten thousand saw I at a glance,
Tossing their heads in sprightly dance.

The waves beside them danced; but they
Out-did the sparkling waves in glee:
A poet could not but be gay,
In such a jocund company;
I gazed – and gazed – but little thought
What wealth the show to me had brought:

For oft, when on my couch I lie
In vacant or in pensive mood,
They flash upon that inward eye
Which is the bliss of solitude;
And then my heart with pleasure fills,
And dances with the daffodils.

In the last stanza, Wordsworth tells how the memory of the daffodils often comes back to him. When we remember events or experiences, general impressions may remain but often details can become lost. Compare the details in Dorothy's description with those in the poem. Are any features different concerning the number of daffodils, their position, their movements? You will notice that

I wandered *lonely* as a cloud

does not conform with the details in the journal, all of which 'we' experienced: he was not lonely. Yet it must be realized that poets may write fiction, and that lines introduced with 'I' can be imagined and not always actual experience.

What are the effects of the altered details in this poem?

*What do you notice about the rhyme scheme and the metre of this poem? (See page 28 on **Rhythm** and page 63 on **Rhyme**.)*

One of Wordsworth's great skills was the ability to write so naturally and in such a regular rhythm that the poetry reads fluently and easily. Write some of your own recollections of early childhood, holidays, memorable visits, any experience which arouses your enthusiasm, either in blank verse pentameters, like ***The Prelude****, or imitating the verse form of* ***The Daffodils****.*

'Poetry has never brought me in enough money to buy shoestrings.'
William Wordsworth

WILLIAM WORDSWORTH

Lines Composed a Few Miles above Tintern Abbey

The sounding cataract
Haunted me like a passion: the tall rock,
The mountain, and the deep and gloomy wood,
Their colours and their forms, were then to me
An appetite; a feeling and a love,
That had no need of a remoter charm,
By thought supplied, nor any interest
Unborrowed from the eye. – That time is past,
And all its aching joys are now no more,
And all its dizzy raptures. Not for this
Faint I, nor mourn nor murmur; other gifts
Have followed; for such loss, I would believe,
Abundant recompense. For I have learned
To look on nature, not as in the hour
Of thoughtless youth; but hearing oftentimes
The still, sad music of humanity,
Nor harsh nor grating, though of ample power
To chasten and subdue. And I have felt
A presence that disturbs me with the joy
Of elevated thoughts; a sense sublime
Of something far more deeply interfused,
Whose dwelling is the light of setting suns,
And the round ocean and the living air,
And the blue sky, and in the mind of man:
A motion and a spirit, that impels
All thinking things, all objects of all thought,
And rolls through all things. Therefore am I still
A lover of the meadows and the woods,
And mountains; and of all that we behold
From this green earth; of all the mighty world
Of eye, and ear, – both what they half create,
And what perceive; well pleased to recognize
In nature and the language of the sense
The anchor of my purest thoughts, the nurse,
The guide, the guardian of my heart, and soul
Of all my moral being.

*Wordsworth commented on the **Lines Composed a Few Miles above Tintern Abbey**: 'No poem of mine was composed under circumstances more pleasant for me to remember than this. I began it upon leaving Tintern, after crossing the Wye, and concluded it just as I was entering Bristol in the evening, after a ramble of four or five days, with my sister. Not a line of it was altered, and not any part of it written down till I reached Bristol.'*

'Poetry is the rock of defence for human nature.'
William Wordsworth

METRE

Metre is a measurement of **rhythm**. Rhythms can be laid down in various patterns, and each different pattern has a name:

Iamb
As in the word **awake** – stress on 2nd syllable of two

Trochee
As in **autumn** – stress on 1st syllable of two

Dactyl
As in **beautiful** – stress on 1st syllable of three

Anapaest
As in **by the hand** – stress on 3rd syllable of three

This is an **Iambic** line:

> My mother wore a yellow dress

So is this:

> It feels a shame to be alive

This is a **Trochaic** line:

> Tiger! Tiger! burning bright

So is this:

> In the forests of the night

A **Dactylic** line:

> Carry her down to the river
> Carry her down to the sea

An **Anapaestic** line:

> In the days we have known one another

As you feel the rhythm of lines of poetry, see if you can find the **metrical pattern** as well, and use patterns of **rhythm** and **metre** in your own writing.

A later Poet Laureate, John Betjeman, also wrote an autobiographical poem, ***Summoned by Bells****, which owes much to Wordsworth in its rhythm and use of sights and sounds. His accounts of events and scenes in his life are very like those of Wordsworth in* ***The Prelude****, but naturally the details and language are modern. The two poets share both an enthusiasm for what they see, and the poetic skill to express their thoughts. Betjeman's poem is written in similar blank verse to Wordsworth's.*

Summoned by Bells

Ears! Hear again the wild sou'westers whine!
Three days on end would the September gale
Slam at our bungalows; three days on end
Rattling cheap doors and making tempers short.
It mattered not, for then enormous waves
House-high rolled thunderous on Greenaway,
Flinging up spume and shingle to the cliffs.
Unmoved amid the foam, the cormorant
Watched from its peak. In all the roar and swirl
The still and small things gained significance.
Somehow the freckled cowrie would survive
And prawns hang waiting in their watery woods;
Deep in the noise there was a core of peace;
Deep in my heart a warm security.
Nose! Smell again the early morning smells:
Congealing bacon and my father's pipe;
The after-breakfast freshness out of doors
Where sun had dried the heavy dew and freed
Acres of thyme to scent the links and lawns;
The rotten apples on our shady path
Where the blowflies settled upon squashy heaps,
Intent and gorging; at the garden gate
Reek of Solignum on the wooden fence;
Mint round the spring, and fennel in the lane,
And honeysuckle wafted from the hedge;
The Lynams' cess-pool like a body-blow;
Then, clean, medicinal and cold – the sea.
'Breathe in the ozone, John. It's iodine.'
But which is iodine and which is drains?
Salt and hot sun on rubber water-wings . . .
Home to the luncheon smell of Irish stew
And washing-up stench from the kitchen sink
Because the sump is blocked. The afternoons
Brought coconut smell of gorse; at Mably's farm
Sweet scent of drying cowdung; then the moist
Exhaling of the earth in Shilla woods –
First earth encountered after days of sand.

Evening brought back the gummy smell of toys
And fishy stink of glue and Stickphast paste,
And sleep inside the laundriness of sheets.
   Eyes! See again the rock-face in the lane,
Years before tarmac and the motor-car.
Across the estuary Stepper Point
Stands, still unquarried, black against the sun;
On its Atlantic face the cliffs fall sheer.
Look down into the weed world of the lawn –
The devil's-coach-horse beetle hurries through,
Lifting its tail up as I bar the way
To further flowery jungles.

John Betjeman

What senses does this Betjeman passage celebrate?

Think about your environment. What sounds, smells, and sights might you remember in thirty years' time?

✤ *Try to imitate Betjeman's style, starting:*

Ears! Hear again . . .
Nose! Smell again . . .
Eyes! See again . . .

An Argument with Wordsworth

'Poetry . . . takes its origin from emotion recollected in tranquility'
Preface to the Lyrical Ballads

People are always quoting that and all of them seem to agree
And it's probably most unwise to admit that it's different for me.
I have emotion – no one who knows me could fail to detect it –
But there's a serious shortage of tranquility in which to recollect it.
So this is my contribution to the theoretical debate:
Sometimes poetry is emotion recollected in a highly emotional state.

Wendy Cope

'Too many people in the modern world view poetry as a luxury, not a necessity, like petrol.'
John Betjeman

Mending Wall

Something there is that doesn't love a wall,
That sends the frozen-ground-swell under it,
And spills the upper boulders in the sun;
And makes gaps even two can pass abreast.
The work of hunters is another thing:
I have come after them and made repair
Where they have left not one stone on a stone,
But they would have the rabbit out of hiding,
To please the yelping dogs. The gaps I mean,
No one has seen them made or heard them made,
But at spring mending-time we find them there.
I let my neighbour know beyond the hill;
And on a day we meet to walk the line
And set the wall between us once again.
We keep the wall between us as we go.
To each the boulders that have fallen to each.
And some are loaves and some so nearly balls
We have to use a spell to make them balance:
'Stand where you are until our backs are turned!'
We wear our fingers rough with handling them.
Oh, just another kind of outdoor game,
One on a side. It comes to little more:
There where it is we do not need the wall:
He is all pine and I am apple-orchard.
My apple trees will never get across
And eat the cones under his pines, I tell him.
He only says, 'Good fences make good neighbours.'
Spring is the mischief in me, and I wonder
If I could put a notion in his head:
'*Why* do they make good neighbours? Isn't it
Where there are cows? But here there are no cows.
Before I built a wall I'd ask to know
What I was walling in or walling out,
And to whom I was like to give offence.
Something there is that doesn't love a wall
That wants it down.' I could say 'Elves' to him,
But it's not elves exactly, and I'd rather
He said it for himself. I see him there,
Bringing a stone grasped firmly by the top
In each hand, like an old-stone savage armed.
He moves in darkness as it seems to me,
Not of woods only and the shade of trees.
He will not go behind his father's saying,
And he likes having thought of it so well
He says again, 'Good fences make good neighbours.'

Robert Frost

Do your thoughts ramble while you are doing a repetitive job? Does this poem ramble? Is there repetition?

✣ *Translate this idea into modern conditions, perhaps working at a check-out in a supermarket, delivering papers, washing up.*

'All the fun's in how you say a thing.'
Robert Frost

Wall

The wall walks the fell –
Grey millipede on slow
Stone hooves;
Its slack back hollowed
At gulleys and grooves,
Or shouldering over
Old boulders
Too big to be rolled away.
Fallen fragments
Of the high crags
Crawl in the walk of the wall.

A dry-stone wall
Is a wall and a wall,
Leaning together
(Cumberland-and-Westmorland
Champion wrestlers),
Greening and weathering,
Flank by flank,
With filling of rubble
Between the two –
A double-rank
Stone dyke:
Flags and through-
stones jutting out sideways,
Like the steps of a stile.

A wall walks slowly.
At each give of the ground,
Each creak of the rock's ribs,
It puts its foot gingerly,
Arches its hog-holes,
Lets cobble and knee-joint
Settle and grip.
As the slipping fellside
Erodes and drifts,
The wall shifts with it,
Is always on the move.

They built a wall slowly,
A day a week;
Built it to stand,
But not stand still.
They built a wall to walk.

Norman Nicholson

What do the first and third stanzas describe the wall as?
This is an example of ***extended metaphor****.*
What is the second stanza about? What metaphor is used here?

✤ *Write extended metaphor poems on street furniture, e.g.: pillar box, telephone kiosk, lamp post, litter bin, road sign.*

Men of Terry Street

They come in at night, leave in the early morning.
I hear their footsteps, the ticking of bicycle chains,
Sudden blasts of motorcycles, whimpering of vans.
Somehow I am either in bed, or the curtains are drawn.

This masculine invisibility makes gods of them,
A pantheon of boots and overalls.
But when you see them, home early from work
Or at their Sunday leisure, they are too tired

And bored to look long at comfortably.
It hurts to see their faces, too sad or too jovial.
They quicken their step at the smell of cooking,
They hold up their children and sing to them.

Are any of these ***extended metaphor*** *poems? What comparisons are being made? What details does Douglas Dunn pick out? Why should he choose these?*

- *Write about:*
  Women of Terry Street
  Arrival in Terry Street
  My Street
  Other people observed in the street: gardeners, bus drivers, shoppers, postmen, traffic wardens, meter readers, window cleaners.

- *Write an extended metaphor poem, e.g.: bus driver as zoo keeper.*

A Removal from Terry Street

On a squeaking cart, they push the usual stuff,
A mattress, bed ends, cups, carpets, chairs,
Four paperback westerns. Two whistling youths
In surplus U.S. Army battle-jackets
Remove their sister's goods. Her husband
Follows, carrying on his shoulders the son
Whose mischief we are glad to see removed,
And pushing, of all things, a lawnmower.
There is no grass in Terry Street. The worms
Come up cracks in concrete yards in moonlight.
That man, I wish him well. I wish him grass.

Douglas Dunn

Pioneers

They service cars, stay with them for hours,
Dipping themselves in gloom, coming up as if for air.
We notice brass doughnut and pagoda leftovers.

Pioneers of Haarlem Road. They have time licked.
They leave untidy parking stationary for weeks
And carry on as if success achieved too early

Would discomfort them. At times we notice them
Inside, doors closed and staring out, as if
The vehicles were home and the world, television.

The White Flag

Each Wednesday morning, they are the masters.
Their vehicles rumble through our streets
Like Russian tanks occupying a foreign capital.

Resoundingly, they storm our properties.
Their sturdy council gloves protect them
From our germs, the breakages not properly wrapped.

A legacy of misplaced bins and fallen lids,
Certain items missed, a carelessness with gates
Show their displeasure, that we must improve.

David Jacobs

Grace for Potato

For the faithful potato we praise thee.
O firm friend, who made potatoes
who made their solid white bodies
their roundness and their strong brown skin
who made them for winter
after you'd made butter, who made their
many eyes, and their full comforting bellies.
You made the potato
on a day when you felt indestructible
when the world's hunger was to be once and for all
cured, under the earth you planted such an abundance
such an overwhelming store of contentment
for the good and faithful potato root
we praise thee, praise thee, praise thee.

Grace for Snow

I prayed to you for sleep, for silence
from the night-voices and peace
from the night-faces.
You sent cloth in thick folds to cover and close
the shiny black eye of the night's window.
I prayed to you for a blessing, for grace
from the slow scream of the city's sorrow.
You sent snow.

Grace for Tomato

For the frail tomato
we praise thee.
In times of fasting
she lies gleaming on the plate
substantial as glass.

In times of plenty she is
blood of the soup
delight of the stew
good friend to onion
a balm to chile and sharp green pepper
astringent cleanser of the greasy
fried egg, that pensioner –
that irritable hunchback
nestling in his symbol
smug as a cliché.
Tomato is his protector.
Tomato is his patron.

From her powdery vines
from her hot fields and distant islands
she comes in shining.
For the frail tomato
rose of africa
we praise thee.

Jeni Couzyn

Talk about the patterns of ***Grace for Potato*** *and* ***Grace for Tomato****.*

✤ *Make a list of the ways in which the two poems are the same, and the ways in which they are different. Look for patterns as you do this.*

Is the pattern of ***Snow*** *like either of them?*

✤ *What are your favourite foods, weathers, entertainments? Write a poem praising one of them.*

'The word has its own substance, and one can hold it, turn it over, feel its weight.'

Jeni Couzyn

Where Innocent Bright-eyed Daisies are

Where innocent bright-eyed daisies are,
With blades of grass between,
Each daisy stands up like a star
Out of a sky of green.

Christina Rossetti

The Fairy Ring

Here the horse-mushrooms make a fairy ring,
Some standing upright and some overthrown,
A small Stonehenge, where heavy black slugs cling
And bite away, like Time, the tender stone.

Andrew Young

How do these two very short poems use change of scale to get their effects? Can both the poems be divided into two parts?

✣ *Use the same pattern to write poems about other everyday things, for example drain covers in the gutter, a TV screen, a bicycle wheel, post coming through the letter box, a dog on a lead.*

October Dawn

October is marigold, and yet
A glass half full of wine left out

To the dark heaven all night, by dawn
Has dreamed a premonition

Of ice across its eye as if
The ice-age had begun its heave.

The lawn overtrodden and strewn
From the night before, and the whistling green

Shrubbery are doomed. Ice
Has got its spearhead into place.

First a skin, delicately here
Restraining a ripple from the air;

Soon plate and rivet on pond and brook;
Then tons of chain and massive lock

To hold rivers. Then, sound by sight
Will Mammoth and Sabre-tooth celebrate

Reunion while a fist of cold
Squeezes the fire at the core of the world,

Squeezes the fire at the core of the heart,
And now it is about to start.

Ted Hughes

What do you notice about the ends of the lines?
Do they rhyme? Do they nearly rhyme?
Are the endings of the lines alike in any way?
***Rhyme** is sometimes used in poetry because its regularity is comforting. What effect do the endings in this poem have on you?*
Do they fit the subject of the poem?

✤ *Try to write about the other end of winter, the gradual arrival of spring. Write in couplets like those in **October Dawn**. Perhaps you could get nearer to rhyme as spring gets a firmer foothold.*

SOUND EFFECTS

The most obvious effects on the sounds of words in poetry are those created by **Rhyme** and by **Rhythm**. But there are some other effects that you should try to notice in the poetry that you read and which you may like to introduce into the poetry that you write:

Alliteration

Sounds of consonants are repeated to produce a sound effect that contributes to the sense, e.g. Wordsworth's description of skating (the 's' and 'sh' sounds sound like skating):

> All *sh*od with *st*eel,
> We hi*ss*'d along the pol*ish*'d ice . . .

Assonance

The vowels 'agree', but consonants do not

> She bid me take life *ea*sy, as the l*ea*ves grow on the tr*ee*

Consonance

Only final consonants 'agree':

> I have learnt more from your li*ps*
> than you will from mine perha*ps*

Onomatopoeia

The sound of the word reflects the sense:

hush   bang   cuckoo

It is often related to **alliteration.** e.g. **hiss'd** (above) is also onomatopoeic.

Thorns

It's usual to dislike them.
Yet what's more friendly?
What says all the time
Stay here. Don't go away?

You prune roses for the roses' sake.
They say *Glory and honour*
as they die in a blue jug.

Their incantation is no less true
than the thorn's message
– that round, red bead
on your startled thumb.

Norman MacCaig

Poems can give a rosy, nostalgic picture of the natural world. Does this one?

Why does the poem use questions?

Compare this poem with **The Sick Rose** *and* **The Lily** *by William Blake on page 14. Are there ways in which they are similar?*

✤ *Write a poem incorporating other less pretty aspects of the countryside, e.g.: flies, battery hens, vast fields, lorry-loads of animals going to slaughter. Balance them against the pretty images.*

On the eleventh day of Christmas my true love sent to me

Eleven Pipers Piping

Eleven shepherds piped around a manger.
Eleven days have passed, and they must take their leave.
Their bagpipe tunes are fading, as they go
Back to the high hills, where linger still
Reverberations of the angels' song.

John Heath-Stubbs

✤ *A Christmas pattern to imitate. There is a complete set of twelve of these that were used for Christmas cards. Try writing others in this series.*

'People say, "How long does it take you to write a poem, Norman?", and I say, "Two cigarettes".'
Norman MacCaig

The Mower, and the five poems that follow it, explore the darker side of the countryside, the death of animals. It is a section to be read as a whole. Talk about the different feelings in the poems, the different images, and the pattern of each poem. How successful is each in telling its story?

The last poem is rather different. Is it meant to be a joke?

✤ *Most of us have mixed feelings when we see dead animals: fascination, horror, sorrow. You could write about a dead pet, or about the animal corpses that litter our roads.*

'I think a young poet, or an old one for that matter, should try to produce something that pleases himself personally, not only when he's written it but a couple of weeks later.'
Philip Larkin

The Mower

The mower stalled, twice; kneeling, I found
A hedgehog jammed up against the blades,
Killed. It had been in the long grass.

I had seen it before, and even fed it, once.
Now I had mauled its unobtrusive world
Unmendably. Burial was no help:

Next morning I got up and it did not.
The first day after a death, the new absence
Is always the same; we should be careful

Of each other, we should be kind
While there is still time.

Philip Larkin

Scything

It is blue May. There is work
to be done. The spring's eye blind
with algae, the stopped water
silent. The garden fills
with nettle and briar.
Dylan drags branches away.
I wade forward with my scythe.

There is stickiness on the blade.
Yolk on my hands. Albumen and blood.
Fragments of shell are baby-bones,
the scythe a scalpel, bloodied and guilty
with crushed feathers, mosses, the cut cords
of the grass. We shout at each other,
each hurting with a separate pain.

From the crown of the hawthorn tree
to the ground the willow warbler
drops. All day in silence she repeats
her question. I too return
to the place holding the pieces,
at first still hot from the knife,
recall how warm birth fluids are.

Gillian Clarke

Interruption to a Journey

The hare we had run over
Bounced about the road
On the springing curve
Of its spine.

Cornfields breathed in the darkness,
We were going through the darkness and
The breathing cornfields from one
Important place to another.

We broke the hare's neck
And made that place, for a moment,
The most important place there was,
Where a bowstring was cut
And a bow broken forever
That had shot itself through so many
Darknesses and cornfields.

It was left in that landscape.
It left us in another.

Norman MacCaig

After Death

Opening up the house
After three weeks away
I found bird droppings
All over the ground floor,
White and heavy on the windows,
On the worktop,
On the cupboards,
On every wild hope of freedom.

I could not find any bird
At first, and feared
Some science fiction mystery,
To be horribly explained
As soon as whatever
It was felt sure
It had got me alone,
A mile from the village.

At last I discovered him,
Weightless and out of the running,
More null than old wrapping paper
A month after Christmas.
No food inside him of course,
He had died of hunger
And no waste either,
He was quite empty.

His desperate ghost
Flew down my throat and my ears.
There was no air
He had not suffered in.
He lay in one place,
His droppings were everywhere
More vivid, more terrible
Than he had been, ever.

Patricia Beer

Dry August Burned

Dry August burned. A harvest hare
Limp on the kitchen table lay,
Its fur blood-blubbered, eyes astare,
While a small child that stood near by
Wept out her heart to see it there.

Sharp came the *clop* of hoofs, the clang
Of dangling chain, voices that rang.
Out like a leveret she ran,
To feast her glistening bird-clear eyes
On a team of field-artillery,
Gay, to manoeuvres, thudding by.
Spur and gun and limber plate
Flashed in the sun. Alert, elate,
Noble horses, foam at lip,
Harness, stirrup, holster, whip,
She watched the sun-tanned soldiery
Till dust-white hedge had hidden away –
Its din into rumour thinned –
The laughing, jolting, wild array;
And then – the wonder and tumult gone –
Stood nibbling a green leaf, alone,
Her dark eyes, dreaming . . . She turned,
and ran,
Elf-like, into the house again.
The hare had vanished . . . 'Mother,' she said,
Her tear-stained cheek now flushed with red,
'Please, may I go and see it skinned?'

Walter de la Mare

Pastoral

I wish I was a provincial poet,
Writing a lot about nature,
Whenever I thought about London poets,
I'd mutter darkly 'I hate yer'.

And off I'd stomp down the wild, wild lanes
In my jeans and my wellington boots.
A provincial poet doesn't need lipstick
Or tights or respectable suits.

The clutter of urban life. How wonderful
Just to discard it all
And spend one's time communing with
everything,
Perched on a dry-stone wall.

And after a busy day communing
To amble back home for a bite,
Then go to the pub with some real people,
Who manage twelve pints in a night,

Which helps them get through the provincial
evenings
Without too much boredom or pain.
Real people, as solid and ruddy and calm
As a London bus in the rain!

Some day I'll go and live in the country
And many a notebook I'll fill
With keen observations of animals (mostly
The dead ones because they keep still).

Dead sheep and squashed rabbits. Oh, how I
shall love it.
My face will be peaceful and brown
And shining with love for all of creation,
Excepting those poets in town.

Wendy Cope

Why Brownlee Left

Why Brownlee left, and where he went,
Is a mystery even now.
For if a man should have been content
It was him; two acres of barley,
One of potatoes, four bullocks,
A milker, a slated farmhouse.
He was last seen going out to plough
On a March morning, bright and early.

By noon Brownlee was famous;
They had found all abandoned, with
The last rig unbroken, his pair of black
Horses, like man and wife,
Shifting their weight from foot to
Foot, and gazing into the future.

Paul Muldoon

With a camera you can take a photo that freezes time, that captures one particular moment. Words can do this too, and we call this a ***snapshot****. In* ***Why Brownlee Left****, which is in sonnet form (see page 80), there is one snapshot in the first part, the octave: two and a half lines that give a quick picture of his farm. The sestet has another: the picture of the horses waiting. It's almost a form of shorthand.*

The Poacher

Turning aside, never meeting
In the still lanes, fly infested,
Our frank greeting with quick smile.
You are the wind that set the bramble
Aimlessly clawing the void air.
The fox knows you, the sly weasel
Feels always the steel comb
Of eyes parting like sharp rain
Among the grasses its smooth fur.
No smoke haunting the cold chimney
Over your hearth betrays your dwelling
In blue writing above the trees.
The robed night, your dark familiar,
Covers your movements; the slick sun,
A dawn accomplice, removes your tracks
One by one from the bright dew.

R. S. Thomas

Why Brownlee Left *and* ***The Poacher*** *are about mysterious people. Both of them use* ***snapshot*** *images. The poacher is like the invisible man; you know he's there but you can't see him. What images are used to create a picture of each?*

✥ *Write about people you know, trying to bring them to life with quick snapshots. What makes them special?*

Solitude

There is a charm in solitude that cheers,
A feeling that the world knows nothing of;
A green delight the wounded mind endears
After the hustling world is broken off,
Whose whole delight was crime – at good to scoff.
Green solitude, his prison, pleasure yields,
The bitch fox heeds him not; birds seem to laugh.
He lives the Crusoe of his lonely field
Whose dark green oaks his noontide leisure shield.

John Clare

The Lake Isle of Innisfree

I will arise and go now, and go to Innisfree,
And a small cabin build there, of clay and wattles made;
Nine bean rows will I have there, a hive for the honey
bee,
And live alone in the bee-loud glade.

And I shall have some peace there, for peace comes
dropping slow,
Dropping from the veils of the morning to where the
cricket sings;
There midnight's all a glimmer, and noon a purple
glow,
And evening full of the linnet's wings.

I will arise and go now, for always night and day
I hear lake water lapping with low sounds by the shore;
While I stand on the roadway, or on the pavements
grey,
I hear it in the deep heart's core.

William Butler Yeats

Here are two ideal, day-dream worlds. Do both poets want to be alone in the country? Do they fear solitude?
How many times does John Clare use the word 'green'? Is it used in the same way each time?
Which of our five senses does Yeats mainly appeal to in his poem?

✤ *What is your day-dream world? Try writing about it.*

You could start:

I will arise and go now, and go to . . .

or

There is a charm in . . .

Both of the poems are about escaping to something or somewhere else. What would you escape from?

✤ *Collect some holiday brochures. Start a poem:*

I will board and fly now, and fly to . . .

Use phrases from the brochures.

✤ *Write an anti-holiday poem using all the things that can go wrong.*

> *'Of our conflicts with others we make rhetoric; of our conflicts with ourselves we make poetry.'*
> W. B. Yeats

Stopping by Woods on a Snowy Evening

Whose woods these are I think I know.
His house is in the village though;
He will not see me stopping here
To watch his woods fill up with snow.

My little horse must think it queer
To stop without a farmhouse near
Between the woods and frozen lake
The darkest evening of the year.

He gives his harness bells a shake
To ask if there is some mistake.
The only other sound's the sweep
Of easy wind and downy flake.

The woods are lovely, dark and deep,
But I have promises to keep,
And miles to go before I sleep,
And miles to go before I sleep.

Robert Frost

This is a poem about one particular moment of frozen time, a time when you look at something and almost go into a trance, feel almost asleep.
What is the **rhyme** *pattern here?*
What effect does this have?
What effect does the repetition have?

Look at the manuscript version of the last three stanzas. There were originally several horses, then only one, and Frost then changed this one horse from male to female and then back to male. What difference do these changes make? Frost wrote later that he repeated the last line as a way out of the problem he had set for himself by his rhyme pattern. Can you see the evidence of this in the manuscript?

✤ *What moment can you remember like this? Can you write in the same trance-like style?*

Hailstorm in May

Strike, churl; hurl, cheerless wind, then; heltering hail
May's beauty massacre and wispèd wild clouds grow
Out on the giant air; tell Summer No,
Bid joy back, have at the harvest, keep Hope pale.

Gerard Manley Hopkins

What is the rhythm of ***Hailstorm****?*
How does it suit the subject?
Read it out loud to emphasize this.
Is ***Thaw*** *different? Does* ***Thaw*** *use a change of scale to gain an effect?*

Thaw

Over the land freckled with snow half-thawed
The speculating rooks at their nests cawed
And saw from elm-tops, delicate as flower of grass,
What we below could not see, Winter pass.

Edward Thomas

✣ *Write a pair of short poems that contrast in the way that these two do. You might choose to write about weather, perhaps, or your moods.*

RHYME

Most people can recognize rhyming words, and these contribute considerably to the **pattern** of a poem. As with **rhythm**, there is an additional satisfaction in speaking or hearing **rhyme** in words. Much appreciation of poetry comes from enjoyment of the sounds of words.

Full Rhyme

Easy to recognize: taking/breaking; spoken one/broken one – this is usually **end-rhyme**, i.e. the end words of a line rhyming.

Partial Rhyme

Often less obvious at once, but has an effect on the sound, the rhythm and the pattern of the words. There are several different forms of **partial** or **imperfect rhyme**:

Internal Rhyme

Rhymes coming in the middle of lines rather than at the end, e.g.

Or sh*ould*ering over
Old b*ould*ers
Too big to be r*olled* away.

Pararhyme

Both consonants agree but the vowel does not, e.g. sipped/supped; mystery/mastery.

Unstressed Rhyme

The rhyming syllable does not fall on the beat (see **Rhythm**), e.g.

I was a nuisance, tripping, falling,
Yapping always.

Eye-Rhyme

Words look similar but are pronounced differently, so do not rhyme fully (though they may have in their original forms) e.g.

move/love; mind/wind; go/do.

A **rhyme scheme** is usually represented by **ABC** to indicate the order of the end-rhymes, e.g.

AABB

I was angry with my friend:	A
I told my wrath, my wrath did end.	A
I was angry with my foe:	B
I told it not, my wrath did grow.	B

ABAB

Only a man harrowing clods	A
In a slow silent walk	B
With an old horse that stumbles and nods	A
Half asleep as they stalk.	B

ABCB

I am Charlotte. I don't say hello	A
to people and sometimes I bite.	B
Although I am dead I still jump	C
out of bed and wake them up at night.	B

Look out for examples of these different forms of **rhyme** as you read the poems, and experiment with them yourself.

D. H. LAWRENCE

D. H. Lawrence was born in 1885, into a poor mining family in Nottinghamshire. He was often ill as a child and his parents quarrelled a lot. His first novel, **Sons and Lovers**, describes his own early life. He worked for a short time as a teacher but illness encouraged him to give it up. After his marriage he and his wife travelled all over the world. He wrote novels, poems, plays, travel books, and essays. He died in 1930, aged 45.

Read through this section. As you read, try to answer these questions:

Is there a common idea running through Lawrence's poems? Are they 'about' the same things? Do they share a common feeling?

❖ *If you have studied the Blake or Wordsworth sections make a list of the different subjects they write about.*

What is special and typical about Lawrence's style? What makes a poem by him different from a poem by, for example, Blake or Wordsworth?

Does Lawrence use the same ***images*** *frequently?*
Do his poems have the same ***pattern****?*
Do they all ***rhyme****, and do they have a regular* ***rhythm****?*

Our Day is Over

Our day is over, night comes up
shadows steal out of the earth.
Shadows, shadows
wash over our knees and splash
  between our thighs,
our day is done;
we wade, we wade, we stagger,
  darkness rushes between our stones,
we shall drown.

Our day is over
night comes up.

Discord in Childhood

Outside the house an ash-tree hung
  its terrible whips,
And at night when the wind rose,
  the lash of the tree
Shrieked and slashed the wind, as a ship's
Weird rigging in a storm shrieks hideously.

Within the house two voices arose,
  a slender lash
Whistling she-delirious rage,
  and the dreadful sound
Of a male thong booming and bruising,
  until it had drowned
The other voice in a silence of blood,
  'neath the noise of the ash.

D. H. LAWRENCE

A Snowy Day in School

All the long school-hours, round the irregular hum of the class
Have pressed immeasurable spaces of hoarse silence
Muffling my mind, as snow muffles the sounds that pass
Down the soiled street. We have pattered the lessons ceaselessly –

But the faces of the boys, in the brooding, yellow light
Have been for me like a dazed constellation of stars,
Like half-blown flowers dimly shaking at the night,
Like half-seen froth on an ebbing shore in the moon.

Out of each face, strange, dark beams that disquiet;
In the open depths of each flower, dark, restless drops;
Twin-bubbling challenge and mystery, in the foam's whispering riot.
– How can I answer the challenge of so many eyes?

The thick snow is crumpled on the roof, it plunges down
Awfully! – Must I call back a hundred eyes? – A voice
Falters a statement about an abstract noun –
What was my question? – My God, must I break this hoarse

Silence that rustles beyond the stars? – There! –
I have startled a hundred eyes, and now I must look
Them an answer back; it is more than I can bear.

The snow descends as if the slow sky shook
In flakes of shadow down; while through the gap
Between the schools sweeps one black rook.

In the playground, a shaggy snowball stands huge and still
With fair flakes lighting down on it. Beyond, the town
Is lost in this shadowed silence the skies distil.

And all things are in silence, they can brood
Alone within the dim and hoarse silence.
Only I and the class must wrangle; this work is a bitter rood!

D. H. LAWRENCE

Last Lesson of the Afternoon

When will the bell ring, and end this weariness?
How long have they tugged the leash, and strained apart,
My pack of unruly hounds! I cannot start
Them again on a quarry of knowledge they hate to hunt,
I can haul them and urge them no more.

No longer now can I endure the brunt
Of the books that lie out on the desks; a full threescore
Of several insults of blotted pages, and scrawl
Of slovenly work that they have offered me.
I am sick, and what on earth is the good of it all?
What good to them or me, I cannot see!

So, shall I take
My last dear fuel of life to heap on my soul
And kindle my will to a flame that shall consume
Their dross of indifference; and take the toll
Of their insults in punishment? – I will not! –

I will not waste my soul and my strength for this.
What do I care for all that they do amiss!
What is the point of this teaching of mine, and of this
Learning of theirs? It all goes down the same abyss.

What does it matter to me, if they can write
A description of a dog, or if they can't?
What is the point? To us both, it is all my aunt!
And yet I'm supposed to care, with all my might.

I do not, and will not; they won't and they don't; and that's all!
I shall keep my strength for myself; they can keep theirs as well.
Why should we beat our heads against the wall
Of each other? I shall sit and wait for the bell.

D. H. LAWRENCE

There is Rain in Me

There is rain in me
running down, running down, trickling
away from memory.

There is ocean in me
swaying, swaying O, so deep
so fathomlessly black
and spurting suddenly up, snow-white, like snow-leopards rearing
high and clawing with rage at the cliffs of the soul
then disappearing back with a hiss
of eternal salt rage; angry is old ocean within a man.

The Sea, the Sea

The sea dissolves so much
and the moon makes away with so much more than we know –
Once the moon comes down
and the sea gets hold of us
cities dissolve like rock-salt
and the sugar melts out of life
iron washes away like an old blood-stain
gold goes out into a green shadow
money makes even no sediment
and only the heart
glitters in salty triumph
over all it has known, that has gone now into salty nothingness.

D. H. LAWRENCE

The Triumph of the Machine

They talk of the triumph of the machine,
but the machine will never triumph.

Out of the thousands and thousands of centuries of man
the unrolling of ferns, white tones of the acanthus lapping at the sun,
for one sad century
machines have triumphed, rolled us hither and thither,
shaking the lark's nest till the eggs have broken.

Shaken the marshes till the geese have gone
and the wild swans flown away singing the swan-song of us.
Hard, hard on the earth the machines are rolling,
but through some hearts they will never roll.

The lark nests in his heart
and the white swan swims in the marshes of his loins,
and through the wide prairies of his breast a young bull herds the cows,
lambs frisk among the daisies of his brain.

And at last
all these creatures that cannot die, driven back
into the innermost corners of the soul
will send up the wild cry of despair.

The trilling lark in a wild despair will trill down from the sky,
the swan will beat the waters in rage, white rage of an enraged swan,
even the lambs will stretch forth their necks like serpents,
like snakes of hate, against the man in the machine:
even the shaking white poplar will dazzle like splinters of glass against him.

D. H. LAWRENCE

And against this inward revolt of the native creatures of the soul
mechanical man, in triumph seated upon the seat of his machine
will be powerless, for no engine can reach into the marshes and depths of a man.

So mechanical man in triumph seated upon the seat of his machine
will be driven mad from himself, and sightless, and on that day
the machines will turn to run into one another
traffic will tangle up in a long-drawn-out crash of collison
and engines will rush at the solid houses, the edifice of our life
will rock in the shock of the mad machine, and the house will come down.

Then, far beyond the ruin, in the far, in the ultimate, remote places
the swan will lift up again his flattened, smitten head,
and look round, and rise, and on the great vaults of his wings
will sweep round and up to greet the sun with a silky glitter of a new day
and the lark will follow trilling, angerless again,
and the lambs will bite off the heads of the daisies for friskiness.
But over the middle of the earth will be the smoky ruin of iron
the triumph of the machine.

D. H. LAWRENCE

Humming-bird

I can imagine, in some otherworld
Primeval-dumb, far back
In that most awful stillness, that only gasped and hummed,
Humming-birds raced down the avenues.

Before anything had a soul,
While life was a heave of Matter, half inanimate,
This little bit chipped off in brilliance
And went whizzing through the slow, vast, succulent stems.

I believe there were no flowers then,
In the world where the humming-bird flashed ahead of creation.
I believe he pierced the slow vegetable veins with his long beak.

Probably he was big
As mosses, and little lizards, they say, were once big.
Probably he was a jabbing, terrifying monster.

We look at him through the wrong end of the long telescope of Time,
Luckily for us.

Destiny

O destiny, destiny,
do you exist, and can a man touch your hand?

O destiny
if I could see your hand, and it were thumbs down,
I would be willing to give way, like the pterodactyl,
and accept obliteration.
I would not even ask to leave a fossil claw extant,
nor a thumb-mark like a clue,
I would be willing to vanish completely, completely.

But if it is thumbs up, and mankind must go on being mankind,
then I am willing to fight, I will roll my sleeves up
and start in.

Only, O destiny
I wish you'd show your hand.

My Enemy

If it is a question of him or me
then down with him!

If he is not with me but against me,
if his presence and his breath are poison to me,
then, if he comes near me
down with him.

Down with him
to the pit of annihilation.

But if he stays far from me, and does not touch me,
he is no longer my concern, he ceases to be
my enemy.

✤ *Here are some suggestions for writing.*

Discord in Childhood
Write your own poem about a quarrel.

Our Day is Over
Could you write a poem entitled 'The Night is Over'?

A Snowy Day in School
Write about a sunny afternoon in school.

Last Lesson of the Afternoon
Lawrence's school poems are written from the point of view of a disillusioned teacher. What would a contented and successful teacher or a fed-up pupil write?

There is Rain in Me
What is in you? A wind, snow, fire, sunshine?

The Triumph of the Machine
Lawrence disliked machines. Write the machines' reply.

Humming-bird
Could you write a similar poem, perhaps about a spider, or a fly buzzing round your room?

My Enemy
Write a poem entitled 'My Friend'.

When you write, try to imitate Lawrence's particular style and his strong feelings.

Keep rereading the poems!

'I like to write when I feel spiteful; it's like having a good sneeze.'
D. H. Lawrence

Parody
On the next two right-hand pages there are parodies of the poems facing them.

from Hiawatha

Then Iagoo, the great boaster,
He the marvellous story-teller,
He the traveller and the talker,
He the friend of old Nokomis,
Made a bow for Hiawatha;
From a branch of ash he made it,
From an oak-bough made the arrows,
Tipped with flint, and winged with feathers,
And the cord he made of deer-skin.
Then he said to Hiawatha –
'Go, my son, into the forest,
Where the red deer herd together,
Kill for us a famous roebuck,
Kill for us a deer with antlers!'

* * *

Hidden in the alder-bushes,
There he waited till the deer came,
Till he saw two antlers lifted,
Saw two eyes look from the thicket,
Saw two nostrils point to windward,
And a deer came down the pathway,
Flecked with leafy light and shadow,
And his heart within him fluttered,
Trembled like the leaves above him,
Like the birch-leaf palpitated,
As the deer came down the pathway.

Then, upon one knee uprising,
Hiawatha aimed an arrow;
Scarce a twig moved with his motion
Scarce a leaf was stirred or rustled,
But the wary roebuck started,
Stamped with all his hoofs together,
Listened with one foot uplifted,
Leaped as if to meet the arrow;
Ah! the singing, fatal arrow,
Like a wasp it buzzed and stung him.
Dead he lay there in the forest,
By the ford across the river;
Beat his timid heart no longer,
But the heart of Hiawatha
Throbbed and shouted and exulted,
As he bore the red deer homeward,
And Iagoo and Nokomis
Hailed his coming with applauses.
From the red deer's hide Nokomis
Made a cloak for Hiawatha,
From the red deer's flesh Nokomis
Made a banquet in his honour.
All the village came and feasted,
All the guests praised Hiawatha,
Called him Strong-Heart, Soan-getaha!
Called him Loon-Heart, Mahn-go-taysee!

H. W. Longfellow

Hiawatha's Mittens

When he killed the Mudjekeewis,
Of the skin he made him mittens,
Made them with the fur side inside,
Made them with the skin side outside,
He, to get the warm side inside,
Put the inside skin side outside;
He, to get the cold side outside,
Put the warm side fur side inside.
That's why he put fur side inside,
Why he put the skin side outside,
Why he turned them inside outside.

Anon.

Hiawatha's Photographing

Finally my Hiawatha
Tumbled all the tribe together,
('Grouped' is not the right expression,)
And, as happy chance would have it,
Did at last obtain a picture
Where the faces all succeeded:
Each came out a perfect likeness.
Then they joined and all abused it,
Unrestrainedly abused it,
As 'the worst and ugliest picture
They could possibly have dreamed of:
Giving one such strange expressions!
Sulkiness, conceit, and meanness!
Really any one would take us
(Any one that did not know us)
For the most unpleasant people!'
(Hiawatha seemed to think so,
Seemed to think it not unlikely.)
All together rang their voices,
Angry, loud, discordant voices,
As of dogs that howl in concert,
As of cats that wail in chorus.

Lewis Carroll

Sea Fever

I must down to the seas again, to the lonely sea and the sky,
And all I ask is a tall ship and a star to steer her by;
And the wheel's kick and the wind's song and the white sail's shaking,
And a grey mist on the sea's face, and a grey dawn breaking.

I must down to the seas again, for the call of the running tide
Is a wild call and a clear call that may not be denied;
And all I ask is a windy day with the white clouds flying,
And the flung spray and the blown spume, and the sea-gulls crying.

I must down to the seas again, to the vagrant gipsy life,
To the gull's way and the whale's way where the wind's like a whetted knife;
And all I ask is a merry yarn from a laughing fellow-rover,
And quiet sleep and a sweet dream when the long trick's over.

John Masefield

If you were judging a parody competition, which of these entries would you give the prize to?

✣ *Try your own parodies of* **Sea Fever** *and* **Hiawatha**. *To do this well you will have to study the originals very carefully.*

'Poets are almost always bald when they get to be about forty.'
John Masefield

April

I must go back to a vest again, to a winter vest with sleeves,
And all I ask is an honest shop where the shop-men are not thieves;
And a fair price, and a free choice, and a full stretch for dining,
And a smooth touch on the bare chest, and a smooth inner lining.

I must go back to a vest again, for that which most I dread
Is a bad cold, a head cold, and a day, or more, in bed;
And all I ask is a friend's advice, and a short time for thinking,
A soft wool, and a man's size, and a good bit for shrinking.

I must go back to a vest again, for the April winds are bleak,
And the spring's way is a cold way, and my circulation weak;
And all I ask, when the cash is paid and we leave the shop together,
Is a warm fire and an armchair, or a change in the weather.

G. F. Bradby

Sea-chill

When Mrs John Masefield and her husband, the author of 'I Must Go Down to the Seas Again', arrived here on a liner, she said to a reporter, 'It was too uppy-downy and Mr Masefield was ill.'
News item

I must go down to the seas again, where the billows romp and reel,
So all I ask is a large ship that rides on an even keel,
And a mild breeze and a broad deck with a slight list to leeward,
And a clean chair in a snug nook and a nice, kind steward.

I must go down to the seas again, the sport of wind and tide,
As the gray wave and the green wave play leapfrog over the side.
And all I want is a glassy calm with a bone-dry scupper,
A good book and a warm rug and a light, plain supper.

I must go down to the seas again, though there I'm a total loss,
And can't say which is worst, the pitch, the plunge, the roll, the toss.
But all I ask is a safe retreat in a bar well tended,
And a soft berth and a smooth course till the long trip's ended.

Arthur Guiterman

Here is a parody of **The Tiger** *by William Blake on page 16.*

O Have you Caught the Tiger

O have you caught the tiger?
   And can you hold him tight?
And what immortal hand or eye
Could frame his fearful symmetry?
   And does he try to bite?

Yes, I have caught the tiger,
   And he was hard to catch.
O tiger, tiger, do not try
To put your tail into my eye,
   And do not bite and scratch.

Yes, I have caught the tiger.
   O tiger, do not bray!
And what immortal hand or eye
Could frame his fearful symmetry
   I should not like to say.

And may I see the tiger?
   I should indeed delight
To see so large an animal
Without a voyage to Bengal.
   And mind you hold him tight.

Yes, you may see the tiger;
   It will amuse you much.
The tiger is, as you will find,
A creature of the feline kind.
   And mind you do not touch.

And do you feed the tiger,
   And do you keep him clean?
He has a less contented look
Than in the Natural History book,
   And seems a trifle lean.

Oh yes, I feed the tiger,
   And soon he will be plump;
I give him groundsel fresh and sweet,
And much canary-seed to eat,
   And wash him at the pump.

It seems to me the tiger
   Has not been lately fed,
Not for a day or two at least;
And that is why the noble beast
   Has bitten off your head.

A. E. Housman

'I could no more define poetry than a terrier could define a rat.'
A. E. Housman

The Jungle Husband

Dearest Evelyn, I often think of you
Out with the guns in the jungle stew
Yesterday I hittapotamus
I put the measurements down for you but they got lost
in the fuss.
It's not a good thing to drink out here
You know, I've practically given it up dear.
Tomorrow I am going alone a long way
Into the jungle. It is all gray
But green on top
Only sometimes when a tree has fallen
The sun comes down plop, it is quite appalling.
You never want to go in a jungle pool
In the hot sun, it would be the act of a fool
Because it's always full of anacondas, Evelyn, not
looking ill-fed
I'll say. So no more now, from your loving husband,
Wilfred.

Stevie Smith

This is a letter poem. Compare it with ***Little Johnny's Final Letter*** *on page 25.*

How is this one different from a real letter? Why are the lines all different lengths? Does it ramble? Why?

✤ *Write the story behind the poem.*

✤ *Write a letter poem in the same style: Evelyn's reply, or your letter home, perhaps from a school trip.*

'Poetry is like a strong explosion in the sky. She makes a mushroom shape of terror and drops to the ground with a strong infection. Also she is a strong way out.'

Stevie Smith

Accidents

The accidents are never happening:
they are too imaginable to be true.
The driver knows his car is still on the road,
heading for Durham in the rain.
The mother knows her baby is just asleep,
curled up with his cuddly blanket, waiting
to be lifted and fed: there's no such thing as cot-death.
The rescue party digging all night in the dunes
can't believe the tunnel has really collapsed:
the children have somehow gone to their Auntie's house;
she has lent them their cousins' pyjamas, they are sitting
giggling together in the big spare room,
pretending to try and spill each other's cocoa.

Fleur Adcock

What is the pattern in this poem?

✤ *What accidents can you describe using* ***snapshots****? Continue the idea in this poem.*

Neighbour

His car sits outside the house.
It never goes anywhere, is it
a pet?

When he goes for this morning paper
he makes a perfect rightangle
at the corner.

What does he do at home? Sit at attention?
Or does he stay in the lobby
like a hatstand?

Does his wife know she married
a diagram? That she goes to bed
with a faded blueprint?

When I meet him
he greets me with a smile
he must have bought somewhere.

His eyes are two teaspoons
that have been emptied
for the last time.

Norman MacCaig

What feeling does the poet have towards his neighbour?
Talk about the pattern of the lines on the page. Do the line breaks help the feeling of the poem?
Why does the writer ask so many questions?
What would the neighbour say?

'Rhythm is of course crucial in poetry, the one essential factor which distinguishes a poem from a set of observations or notes.'
Fleur Adcock

Baby-sitting

I am sitting in a strange room listening
For the wrong baby. I don't love
This baby. She is sleeping a snuffly
Roseate, bubbling sleep; she is fair;
She is a perfectly acceptable child.
I am afraid of her. If she wakes
She will hate me. She will shout
Her hot, midnight rage, her nose
Will stream disgustingly and the perfume
Of her breath will fail to enchant me.

To her I will represent absolute
Abandonment. For her it will be worse
Than for the lover cold in lonely
Sheets; worse than for the woman who waits
A moment to collect her dignity
Beside the bleached bone in the terminal ward.
As she rises sobbing from the monstrous land
Stretching for milk-familiar comforting,
She will find me and between us two
It will not come. It will not come.

Gillian Clarke

What feeling does the baby-sitter in the poem have? Have you been baby-sitting? If so, did you have the same feeling?
What images does Gillian Clarke use?

How does the baby feel, and the baby's mother?
What situations make you feel ill at ease?

'You can't be a poet if you don't use your senses properly.'
Gillian Clarke

VERSE FORMS

A **stanza** (Italian for 'stopping place') is a grouping of the verse-lines in a poem, marked off by a space in the printed text. Poems are divided into 'stanzas', sometimes called 'verses'.

A **couplet** is a pair of rhymed lines, e.g.

> What is this life if, full of care,
> We have no time to stand and stare?

A **tercet**, or **triplet**, is a stanza of three lines, usually with a single rhyme; an example of a poem written in triplets is **Do not Go Gentle into that Good Night** by Dylan Thomas. This poem is also in the form of a **villanelle**, a metrical form from medieval French Provence. It consists of five **triplets** and a **quatrain**, all on two rhymes.

A **quatrain**, or four-line stanza, is the most common in English poetry; you will find many examples of poems written in quatrains in this book.

A **haiku** (e.g. **The Canticle of the Sun**) is a Japanese verse form, consisting of 17 syllables over three lines of five syllables/seven syllables/five syllables.

A **sonnet** is a rigid verse form. Originally it was a lyric poem written in fourteen iambic pentameters (see pages 28 and 43 on **rhythm** and **metre**), with an intricate rhyme scheme (see page 63 on **rhyme**). In English poetry the rhyme in a sonnet usually follows one of two patterns:

a The 'Italian' sonnet falls into two main parts: the **octave** consisting of 8 lines rhyming **ABBA, ABBA** and a **sestet** (6 lines) rhyming **CDECDE**;

b The 'English' or 'Shakespearean' sonnet falls into three **quatrains** and a **couplet**, rhyming **ABAB CDCD EFEF GG**.

ROGER McGOUGH

'I was born in Liverpool and began writing poems when I was eighteen. After University I toiled as a teacher for three and a half years before leaving to form **The Scaffold** (a poetry, humour, music group who had a No. 1 hit in 1968 with **Lily The Pink**). Since the mid-seventies I have lived in London and worked as a poet, publishing books for both adults and children. When not writing I travel the known world reading my poems.'

Hundreds and Thousands

The sound of hounds
on red sand thundering

Hundreds and thousands
of mouths glistening

The blood quickening
Thunder and lightning

The hunted in dread
of the hundreds running

The sound of thunder
A white moon reddening

Thousands of mad hounds
on red sand marauding

Thundering onwards
in hundreds and thundreds

Thundreds and thundreds
Thundering   Thundering

'I was asked to write a poem in aid of the N.S.P.C.C.'s 100th birthday and the word 'hundred' had to be in the title. At the top of my page I wrote 'hundredsandthousands' and forgetting the meaning looked at the words and sounds that it contained. For instance "sand", "red", "dred" (i.e. dread), "hun", "hou––nds". I let the images and the sound of the words dictate the poem.'

ROGER McGOUGH

The Identification

So you think its Stephen?
Then I'd best make sure
Be on the safe side as it were.
Ah, theres been a mistake. The hair
you see, its black, now Stephens fair . . .
Whats that? The explosion?
Of course, burnt black. Silly of me.
I should have known. Then lets get on.

The face, is that the face I ask?
that mask of charred wood
blistered, scarred could
that have been a child's face?
The sweater, where intact, looks
in fact all too familiar.
But one must be sure.

The scoutbelt. Yes thats his.
I recognise the studs he hammered in
not a week ago. At the age
when boys get clothes-conscious
now you know. Its almost
certainly Stephen. But one must
be sure. Remove all trace of doubt.
Pull out every splinter of hope.

Pockets. Empty the pockets.
Handkerchief? Could be any schoolboy's.
Dirty enough. Cigarettes?
Oh this can't be Stephen.
I don't allow him to smoke you see.
He wouldn't disobey me. Not his father.
But thats his penknife. Thats his alright.

And thats his key on the keyring
Gran gave him just the other night.
Then this must be him.

I think I know what happened
. . . . about the cigarettes
No doubt he was minding them
for one of the older boys.
Yes thats it.
Thats him.
Thats our Stephen.

'Several years ago in Belfast, a bomb exploded in the Abercorn Restaurant, killing and wounding many children. On television that night, a father talked calmly about the dreadful experience of having to identify the body of his son. I was very moved by his heartbreaking account and wanted to write something that expressed the anger, loss and futility that he felt. I began the poem in note form and then could go no further. It was not until months later when rewriting that I came to the idea of the cigarettes. The idea of a father clinging on to the unreal, but preferred image of his son, opened up the poem and gave it a voice.'

ROGER McGOUGH

A Cautionary Calendar

Beware January,
His greeting is a grey chill.
Dark stranger. First in at the kill.
Get out while you can.

Beware February,
Jolly snowman. But beneath the snow
A grinning skeleton, a scarecrow.
Don't be drawn into that web.

Beware March,
Mad Piper in a many-coloured coat
Who will play a jig then rip your throat.
If you leave home, don't go far.

Beware April,
Who sucks eggs and tramples nests.
From the wind that molests
There is no escape.

Beware May,
Darling scalpel, gall and wormwood.
Scented blossom hides the smell
Of blood. Keep away.

Beware June,
Black lipstick, bruise-coloured rouge,
Sirensong and subterfuge.
The wide-eyed crazed hypnotic moon.

Beware July,
Its juices overflow. Lover of excess
Overripe in flyblown dress.
Insatiable and cruel.

Beware August,
The finger that will scorch and blind
Also beckons. The only place you will find
To cool off is the morgue.

Beware September,
Who speaks softly with honeyed breath.
You promise fruitfulness. But death
Is the only gift that she'll accept.

Beware October,
Whose scythe is keenest. The old crone
Makes the earth tremble and moan.
She's mean and won't be mocked.

Beware November,
Whose teeth are sharpened on cemetery stones,
Who will trip you up and crunch your bones.
Iron fist in iron glove.

Beware December,
False beard that hides a sneer.
Child-hater. In what year
Will we know peace?

'Having received a New Year's calendar with the usual pictorial representations of the coming year – snowman, bonfires, buckets and spades etc. – I wanted to write a dark poem full of foreboding in the manner of a medieval masque.

'One difficult but interesting problem arose when I decided to rhyme the last word in each quatrain with the first syllable of the month. Easy for June, less so for November.'

ROGER McGOUGH

'I enjoy drawing and this began life as a cartoon. I was thinking of how society condones, even applauds certain kinds of killing while being affronted by others. Thinking about the words "fish", "to fish", "fishing", "fisherman" led me to explore "bird", "to bird", "birding", "birder" (which sounds like "murder") and finally "birderman". And so to the chilling birderman, who in his matter-of-fact way chooses which creatures shall live and which shall die.'

The Birderman

Most weekends, starting in the spring
Until late summer, I spend angling.
Not for fish. I find that far too tame
But for birds, a much more interesting game.

A juicy worm I use as bait
Cast a line into the tree and wait.
Seldom for long (that's half the fun)
A commotion in the leaves, the job's half done.

Pull hard, jerk home the hook
Then reel him in. Let's have a look . . .
A tiny thing, a fledgling, young enough to spare.
I show mercy. Unhook, and toss it to the air.

It flies nestwards and disappears among the leaves
(What man roasts and braises, he too reprieves).
What next? A magpie. Note the splendid tail.
I wring its neck. Though stringy, it'll pass for quail.

Unlike water, the depths of trees are high
So, standing back, I cast into the sky.
And ledger there beyond the topmost bough,
Until threshing down, like a black cape, screams a crow!

Evil creature! A witch in feathered form.
I try to net the dark, encircling storm.
It caws for help. Its cronies gather round
They curse and swoop. I hold my ground.

An infernal mass, a black, horrific army
I'll not succumb to Satan's origami.
I reach into my coat, I've come prepared,
Bring out my pocket scarecrow – Watch out bird!

It's cross-shaped, the sign the godless fear
In a thunderflap of wings they disappear.
Except of course, that one, ungainly kite
Broken now, and quickly losing height.

I haul it in, and with a single blow
Dispatch it to that Aviary below.
The ebb and flow: magpie, thrush, nightingale and crow.
The wood darkens. Time to go.

I pack away the food I've caught
And thankful for a good day's sport
Amble home. The forest fisherman.
And I'll return as soon as I can

To bird. For I'm a birderer. The birderman.

ROGER McGOUGH

Hearts and Flowers

Aunty Marge,
Spinster of the parish, never had a boyfriend.
Never courted, never kissed.
A jerrybuilt dentist and a smashed jaw
Saw to that.

To her,
Life was a storm in a holy-water font
Across which she breezed
With all the grace and charm
Of a giraffe learning to windsurf.

But sweating
In the convent laundry, she would iron
Amices, albs and surplices
With such tenderness and care
You'd think priests were still inside.

Deep down,
She would like to have been a nun
And talked of missing her vocation
As if it were the last bus home:
'It passed me by when I was looking the other way.'

'Besides,'
She'd say, 'What Order would have me?
The Little Daughters of the Woodbine?
The Holy Whist Sisters?' A glance at the ceiling.
'He's not that hard up.'

We'd laugh
And protest, knowing in our hearts that He wasn't.
But for the face she would have been out there,
Married, five kids, another on the way.
Celibacy a gift unearned, unasked for.

But though
A goose among grown-ups,
Let loose among kids
She was an exploding fireworks factory,
A runaway pantomime horse.

Everybody's
Favourite aunt. A cuddly toy adult
That sang loud and out of tune.

That dropped, knocked over and bumped into things,
That got ticked off just like us.

Next to
A game of cards she liked babysitting best.
Once the parents were out of the way
It was every child for itself. In charge,
Aunt Marge, renegade toddler-in-chief.

Falling
Asleep over pontoon, my sister and I,
Red-eyed, would beg to be taken to bed.
'Just one more game of snap,' she'd plead,
And magic two toffees from behind an ear.

Then suddenly
Whooshed upstairs in the time it takes
To open the front door. Leaving us to possum,
She'd tiptoe down with the fortnightly fib:
'Still fast asleep, not a murmur all night. Little angels.'

But angels
Unangelic, grew up and flew away. And fallen,
Looked for brighter toys. Each Christmas sent a card
With kisses, and wondered how she coped alone.
Up there in a council flat. No phone.

Her death
Was as quick as it was clumsy. Neighbours
Found the body, not us. Sitting there for days
Stiff in Sunday best. Coat half-buttoned, hat askew.
On her way to Mass. Late as usual.

Her rosary
Had snapped with the pain, the decades spilling,
Black beads trailing. The crucifix still
Clenched in her fist. Middle finger broken.
Branded into dead flesh, the sign of the cross.

From the missal
In her lap, holy pictures, like playing cards,
Lay scattered. Five were face-up:
A Full House of Sacred Hearts and Little Flowers.
Aunty Marge, lucky in cards.

The Boyhood of Raleigh

After the painting by Millais

Entranced, he listens to salty tales
Of derring-do and giant whales,

Uncharted seas and Spanish gold,
Tempests raging, pirates bold.

And his friend? 'God, I'm bored.
As for Jolly Jack I don't believe a word.

What a way to spend the afternoon –
the stink of fish, and those ghastly pantaloons!'

*'**The Boyhood of Raleigh** is a poem that was written to order. The Tate Gallery in London, wishing to explore the relationships between poetry and the visual arts, invited a number of poets to write poems inspired by paintings or pieces of sculpture in The Tate.*

'I chose one of the most popular paintings to be found there, the one by Millais. Looking at it I wondered about the second boy. Who was he? What became of him? Is it a history lesson? Is it a geography lesson? Certainly it is a Friday afternoon.'

The Examination

'Usually once a year, if I am lucky, I am invited by the Arvon Foundation to be a tutor on one of their Poetry Writing Courses. Part of the course entails discussing students' work on a one-to-one basis. This can be a daunting experience for first-timers, and the sessions are sometimes referred to as "writing surgeries".'

'Well doctor, what do you think?'
He took the poem and examined it.
'Mmmm . . .'
The clock ticked nervously.
'This will have to come out for a start.'
He stabbed a cold finger into its heart.
'Needs cutting here as well.
This can go.
And this is weak. Needs building up.'
He paused . . .
'But it's the Caesura I'm afraid,
Can't do much about that.'
My palms sweated.
'Throw it away and start again, that's my advice.
And on the way out, send in the next patient, will you?'

I buttoned up my manuscript and left.
Outside, it was raining odes and stanzas.
I caught a crowded anthology and went directly home.

Realizing finally that I would never be published,
That I was to remain one of the alltime great unknown poets,
My work rejected by even the vanity presses,
I decided to end it all.

Taking an overdose of Lyricism
I awaited the final peace
When into the room burst the Verse Squad
Followed by the Poetry Police.

ROGER McGOUGH

Tramp Tramp Tramp

Insanity left him when he needed it most.
Forty years at Bryant & May, and a scroll
To prove it. Gold lettering, and a likeness
Of the Founder. Grandad's name writ small:
'William McGarry, faithful employee'.

A spent match by the time I knew him.
Choking on fish bones, talking to himself,
And walking round the block with a yardbrush
Over his shoulder. 'What for, Gran?' 'Hush ...
Poor man, thinks he's marching off to war.

'Spitting image of Charlie, was your Grandad,
And taller too.' She'd sigh. 'Best-looking
Man in Seaforth. And straight-backed?
Why, he'd walk down Bridge Road
As if he had a coat-hanger in his suit.'

St Joseph's Hospice for the Dying, in Kirkdale,
Is where Chaplin made his last movie.
He played Grandad, and gave a fine performance
Of a man raging against God, and cursing
Nuns and nurses who tried to hold him down.

Insanity left him when he needed it most.
The pillow taken from his face
At the moment of going under. Screaming
And fighting to regain the years denied,
His heart gave out, his mind gave in, he died.

The final scene brings tears to everybody's eyes.
In the parlour, among suppurating candles
And severed flowers, I see him smiling
Like I'd never seen him smile before.
Coat-hanger at his back. Marching off to war.

'My only memories of my maternal grandfather are not happy ones. He was mentally depressive, a sad, shuffling figure. My grandmother described him when young, as looking like an off-screen Charlie Chaplin – blue eyes, black curly hair, moustache – hence the tramp in the title (also as in marching off to war). For years cushioned from reality, as death approached the mental illness lifted, putting him in touch with his situation and the realization of the years lost.'

In Time of 'The Breaking of Nations' (1915)

I

Only a man harrowing clods
  In a slow silent walk
With an old horse that stumbles and nods
  Half asleep as they stalk.

II

Only thin smoke without flame
  From the heaps of couch-grass;
Yet this will go onward the same
  Though Dynasties pass.

III

Yonder a maid and her wight
  Come whispering by;
War's annals will cloud into night
  Ere their story die.

Thomas Hardy

The idea that love is always with us is conveyed in this poem about war. This and the following poem, **In Memoriam** *(also written in 1915), both show that the reality of the Great War was dawning on people at this time.*

In line 11 of this poem Hardy wrote 'fade' as an alternative to 'cloud'. Which is better?

Each of these poems uses a single **image** *(see page 36) to express the loss of friends in war.*

✤ *Try to produce a* **pastiche** *of the Edward Thomas poem, using your own single image to express a feature of war.*

In Memoriam

(Easter, 1915)

The flowers left thick at nightfall in the wood
This Eastertide call into mind the men
Now far from home, who, with their sweethearts
  should
Have gathered them and will never do again.

Edward Thomas

> *'Poetry is emotion put into measure. The emotion must come by nature, but the measure can be acquired by art.'*
> *Thomas Hardy*

The five poems which follow express in different ways the effect of war on individuals. Often the consequences of war are shown in terms of statistics and the effects on thousands – these concentrate on single friends or relations.

Vergissmeinnicht

Three weeks gone and the combatants gone,
returning over the nightmare ground
we found the place again, and found
the soldier sprawling in the sun.

The frowning barrel of his gun
overshadowing. As we came on
that day, he hit my tank with one
like the entry of a demon.

Look. Here in the gunpit spoil
the dishonoured picture of his girl
who has put: *Steffi. Vergissmeinnicht*
in a copybook gothic script.

We see him almost with content,
abased, and seeming to have paid
and mocked at by his own equipment
that's hard and good when he's decayed.

But she would weep to see today
how on his skin the swart flies move;
the dust upon the paper eye
and the burst stomach like a cave.

For here the lover and killer are mingled
who had one body and one heart.
And death who had the soldier singled
has done the lover mortal hurt.

Keith Douglas

The Lover

Three weeks gone and the combatants gone,
returning over the nightmare ground
we found the place again, and found
the soldier sprawling in the sun.

The frowning barrel of the gun
overshadows him – as we came on
that day, he hit my tank with one,
it was like the entry of a demon.

And smiling in the gunpit spoil
the soiled picture of his girl
who has written: Steffi, Vergissmeinnicht
in a copybook gothic script.

We see him, almost with content
abased, and seeming to have paid
and mocked at by his own equipment
that's durable when he's decayed.

But she would weep to see today
how on his skin the swart flies move;
the dust upon the paper eye
and the burst stomach like a cave.

For here the lover and killer are mingled
having one body and one heart;
here Death, who had the soldier singled,
has done the lover mortal hurt.

Tunisia 1943

Mein Mund ist stumm, aber mein Aug'es spricht
Und was es sagt ist kurz – Vergissmeinnicht.

Steffi

The Lover *is an earlier draft of* ***Vergissmeinnicht****.*

Vergissmeinnicht *means 'forget me not' in German. As well as* ***The Lover****, Douglas used another title for the poem,* ***Elegy for an 88 Gunner****. Discuss which title you think is the most appropriate.*

Compare the third stanzas:

> And smiling in the gunpit spoil
> the soiled picture of his girl
> who has written . . .

has become

> Look. Here in the gunpit spoil
> the dishonoured picture of his girl
> who has put . . .

Discuss the changes he has made – are they more effective?

The dead soldier's equipment has changed from 'durable' to 'hard and good'. This is simpler, but is it better?

Find examples of ***full rhyme*** *and* ***partial rhyme*** *in the final version (**see page 63 on* ***rhyme****).*

✤ *Write a poem that Steffi might have composed (but in English).*

To Lucasta, Going to the Wars

Tell me not, Sweet, I am unkind,
  That from the nunnery
Of thy chaste breast, and quiet mind,
  To war and arms I fly.

True; a new mistress now I chase,
  The first foe in the field;
And with a stronger faith embrace
  A sword, a horse, a shield.

Yet this inconstancy is such
  As thou too shalt adore;
I could not love thee, Dear, so much,
  Loved I not Honour more.

Richard Lovelace

Lovelace is making the choice between his loved one and the glories of war. What **rhythm** *and* **rhyme schemes** *are used here?* *(See pages 28 and 63.)*

✜ *Write a pastiche of this poem, following the same verse form and rhyme scheme, as a response from Lucasta, who does not want him to go to war.*

Ultima Ratio Regum

The guns spell money's ultimate reason
In letters of lead on the Spring hillside.
But the boy lying dead under the olive trees
Was too young and too silly
To have been notable to their important eye.
He was a better target for a kiss.

When he lived, tall factory hooters never summoned
him
Nor did restaurant plate-glass doors revolve to wave
him in.
His name never appeared in the papers.
The world maintained its traditional wall
Round the dead with their gold sunk deep as a well,
Whilst his life, intangible as a Stock Exchange rumour,
drifted outside.

O too lightly he threw down his cap
One day when the breeze threw petals from the trees.
The unflowering wall sprouted with guns,
Machine-gun anger quickly scythed the grasses;
Flags and leaves fell from hands and branches;
The tweed cap rotted in the nettles.

Consider his life which was valueless
In terms of employment, hotel ledgers, news files.
Consider. One bullet in ten thousand kills a man.
Ask. Was so much expenditure justified
On the death of one so young, and so silly
Lying under the olive trees, O world, O death?

Stephen Spender

Ultima Ratio Regum *(meaning 'the kings' ultimate reason' in Latin) is a* ***snapshot*** *of a young boy killed in war. Write your own expression of the waste of a young life, perhaps as the result of a terrorist bomb.*

'Great poetry is always written by somebody straining to go beyond what he can do.'
Stephen Spender

Frustration

Move him into the sun.
~~Gently~~
~~Let us~~ ~~move him to the warm sun~~

Its
~~Whose~~ touch awoke him ~~gently~~ once
In Wales, whispering of fields unsown.
It broke his sleep, today in France.
If anything might rouse him now
The kindly sun will know.

it
Think how ~~then the sun~~
~~its shine~~ awakes the grain.
Woke even the sands of a cold star.
Is youth harder to raise, full-grown,
Still whole, still warm? – He does not stir.

sunbeams
I wonder why the ~~epochs~~ toil
To make us hearts at all.

Why did the suns of epoch toil
To make us hearts at all?

Futility

Move him into the sun. –
~~and his brow's snow~~
~~The snow will melt – soon~~
Gently its touch awoke him once,
~~Easily called him to~~
~~At home whispering of~~ fields
half-sown.
Called him out to
Always it woke him, even in
France,
Until this morning and this snow.
If anything might rouse him now
The kind old sun will know.

Think how it wakes the seeds, –
Woke, once, the clays of a cold star.
Are ~~almost~~
~~Yet~~ ~~Are~~ limbs, perfect ~~at last~~, and sides
~~And heart still warm it cannot~~
~~Almost~~ life-warm ~~too hard to~~ stir ~~?.~~
Full nerved, still warm too hard
Was it for this the clay grew tall?
fatuous
O ~~O~~ What ~~fatuity~~ made ~~the~~ sun ~~toil~~
beams toil
To break earth's sleep at all?

bled
Are limbs ~~pricked~~ with a little
sword,
Yet limbs – still warm – too hard to
stir?
Are limbs, ~~so~~ ready for life, full
grown,
Nerved and still warm, too
hard to stir?

Futility

Move him into the sun. –
Gently its touch awoke him once,
At home, whispering of fields unsown.
Always it woke him, even in France,
Until this morning and this snow.
If anything might rouse him now
The kind old sun will know.

Think how it wakes the seeds, –
Woke, once, the clays of a cold star.
Are limbs, so dear-achieved, are sides,
Full-nerved – still warm – too hard to stir?
Was it for this the clay grew tall?
O what made fatuous sunbeams toil
To break earth's sleep at all?

Wilfred Owen

Here is another example of draft-writing. Owen worked with great attention to detail over this poem – do you feel his final version was the most effective?

Discuss the details of his drafts and what you feel about his alterations. Is ***Futility*** *a better title than* ***Frustration****? Does the poem lose anything by the removal of the 'snow' image from the second draft?*

Whose touch awoke him gently once

has become

gently its touch awoke him once

Is this better in terms of rhythm and expression?

I wonder why the sunbeams toil

has become

O what made fatuous sunbeams toil,

and

the kindly sun

has become

the kind old sun

What are the effects of these changes?

'All the poet can do today is warn. That is why the true Poets must be truthful.'
Wilfred Owen

Post-war

In 1943
my father
dropped bombs on the continent

I remember
my mother
talking about bananas
in 1944

when it rained,
creeping alone to the windowsill,
I stared up the hill,
watching, watching,
watching without a blink
for the Mighty Bananas
to stride through the blitz

they came in paper bags
in neighbours' hands
when they came
and took their time
over the coming

and still I don't know
where my father
flying home
took a wrong turning

Libby Houston

***Post-war** is about the death of the poet's father, but also about memories of early childhood.*

❖ *Small things take on great significance at that age. Can you remember things which seemed very important to you when you were young, which you now realize were trivial? Write about them.*

*'I was quite interested in the comment ... (above, by the authors) – which wasn't my point at all; because I didn't **know** a banana was a small thing – I didn't know what it was at all, except my mother and others did talk about them – "When the war's over, the banana boats will get through at last." So I found them mystifyingly trivial then, when they **did** get through – when I was 4 or so. And I think my mother didn't talk about my father, you see.'* (Libby Houston)

'I think it is the music in poetry I love most of all – how heard words act together, sometimes fighting, sometimes running hand in hand ...'
Libby Houston

Base Details

If I were fierce, and bald, and short of breath,
   I'd live with scarlet Majors at the Base,
And speed glum heroes up the line to death.
   You'd see me with my puffy petulant face,
Guzzling and gulping in the best hotel,
   Reading the Roll of Honour. 'Poor young chap,'
I'd say – 'I used to know his father well;
   Yes, we've lost heavily in this last scrap.'
And when the war is done and youth stone dead,
   I'd toddle safely home and die – in bed.

Siegfried Sassoon wrote a great deal of poetry on war. These poems are ***snapshots*** *(see page 59) of two features which disturbed him most: the awful suffering of individuals and the apparent callousness of the officers.*

❖ *Try writing your own eight-line snapshots of, for example, a politician in the nuclear age, a terrorist, a victim of terrorism, a leader vulnerable to assassination.*

The General

'Good-morning, good-morning!' the General said
When we met him last week on our way to the line.
Now the soldiers he smiled at are most of 'em dead,
And we're cursing his staff for incompetent swine.
'He's a cheery old card,' grunted Harry to Jack
As they slogged up to Arras with rifle and pack.

But he did for them both by his plan of attack.

The Dug-out

Why do you lie with your legs ungainly huddled,
And one arm bent across your sullen, cold,
Exhausted face? It hurts my heart to watch you,
Deep-shadow'd from the candle's guttering gold;
And you wonder why I shake you by the shoulder;
Drowsy, you mumble and sigh and turn your head . . .
You are too young to fall asleep for ever;
And when you sleep you remind me of the dead.

St Venant, July 1918.

Siegfried Sassoon

Ballad of the Faithless Wife

Carry her down to the river
  Carry her down to the sea
Let the bully-boys stare at her braided hair
  But never a glance from me.

Down by the writhing water
  Down by the innocent sand
They laid my bride by the toiling tide
  A stone in her rifled hand.

Under the dainty eagle
  Under the ravening dove
Under a high and healthy sky
  I waited for my love.

Off she ran with a soldier
  Tall as a summer tree,
Soft as a mouse he came to my house
  And stole my love from me.

O splintered were all the windows
  And broken all the chairs
War like a knife ran through my life
  And the blood ran down the stairs.

Loud on the singing morning
  I hear the mad birds rise
Safe from harm to the sun's alarm
  As the sound of fighting dies.

I would hang my harp on the branches
  And weep all through the day
But stranger, see! The wounded tree
  Has burned itself away.

False O false was my lover
  Dead on the diamond shore
White as a fleece, for her name was Peace
  And the soldier's name was War.

Charles Causley

*Ballad of the Faithless Wife is a poem of war, but it uses an unusual, surprising **image** so that the reader does not realize what the **extended metaphor** represents until the end.*

Can you think of an unusual image to express a feature of war?

✣ *Try writing a similar poem, leaving the surprise explanation until the end, as Causley has done.*

'The "idea" for a poem is always a bit vague ... The writing of the poem is a kind of disentangling process to try and discover what the idea is really about.'
Charles Causley

It Feels a Shame to be Alive

It feels a shame to be Alive –
When Men so brave – are dead –
One envies the Distinguished Dust –
Permitted – such a Head –

The Stone – that tells defending Whom
This Spartan put away
What little of Him we – possessed
In Pawn for Liberty –

The price is great – Sublimely paid –
Do we deserve – a Thing –
That lives – like Dollars – must be piled
Before we may obtain?

Are we that wait – sufficient worth –
That such Enormous Pearl
As life – dissolved be – for Us –
In Battle's – horrid Bowl?

It may be – a Renown to live –
I think the Men who die –
Those unsustained – Saviours –
Present Divinity –

Emily Dickinson

Emily Dickinson had a very distinctive style – she wrote hundreds of poems in this ***pattern****, separating ideas with dashes and following a regular* ***rhythm****.*

Find what the rhythm is *(see page 28).*

✤ *Write a poem in imitation of her style on a subject of your choice.*

> *'If I feel physically as if the top of my head were taken off, I know that is poetry.'*
>
> *Emily Dickinson*

A War Film

I saw,
With a catch of the breath and the heart's uplifting,
Sorrow and pride,
   The 'week's great draw' –
The Mons Retreat;
The 'Old Contemptibles' who fought, and died,
The horror and the anguish and the glory.

As in a dream,
Still hearing machine-guns rattle and shells scream,
I came out into the street.

When the day was done,
My little son
Wondered at bath-time why I kissed him so,
Naked upon my knee.
How could he know
The sudden terror that assaulted me? . . .
The body I had borne
Nine moons beneath my heart,
A part of me . . .
If, someday,
It should be taken away
To War. Tortured. Torn.
Slain.
Rotting in No Man's Land, out in the rain –
My little son . . .
Yet all those men had mothers, every one.

How should he know
Why I kissed and kissed and kissed him, crooning his name?
He thought that I was daft.
He thought it was a game,
And laughed, and laughed.

Teresa Hooley

The Projectionist's Nightmare

This is the projectionist's nightmare:
A bird finds its way into the cinema,
finds the beam, flies down it,
smashes into a screen depicting a garden,
a sunset and two people being nice to each other.
Real blood, real intestines, slither down
the likeness of a tree.
'This is no good,' screams the audience.
'This is not what we came to see.'

Brian Patten

The Projectionist's Nightmare *and* ***A War Film*** *both deal with film as against reality.*

✣ *Many war films glamorize war and fighting and killing – write your own poem to show how a war film you have seen has the wrong slant on the subject.*

War Blinded

For more than sixty years he has been blind
Behind that wall, these trees, with terrible
Longevity wheeled in the sun and wind
On pathways of the soldiers' hospital.

For half that time his story's troubled me –
That showroom by the ferry, where I saw
His basketwork, a touch-turned filigree
His fingers coaxed from charitable straw;

Or how he felt when young, enlisting at
Recruiting tables on the football pitch,
To end up slumped across a parapet,
His eye-blood running in a molten ditch;

Or how the light looked when I saw two men,
One blind, one in a wheelchair, in that park,
Their dignity, which I have not forgotten,
Which helps me struggle with this lesser dark.

That war's too old for me to understand
How he might think, nursed now in wards of want,
Remembering that day when his right hand
Gripped on the shoulder of the man in front.

Douglas Dunn

War leads to maiming and disability. Blindness is a disability which those who can see find it difficult to imagine. (What would Wordsworth's descriptions have been like if he had been blind?) Yet it leads to a sharpening of the imagination in those who are blind.

War Blinded *is a carefully constructed poem. It has regular* ***rhythm*** *and* ***rhyme****: can you describe the* ***rhythm*** *and* ***rhyme schemes****?* *(See pages 28 and 63.)* *There are also many examples of* ***enjambement****, where the sense of one line runs on into the next without pause, e.g.*

> where I saw/His basketwork
> enlisting at/Recruiting tables.

✣ *Imagine features of life for a blind person – it could be yourself – and write your own poem. You can try to imitate this style, in which the rhyme at the end of the line does not necessarily mean the end of the idea.*

On his Blindness

When I consider how my light is spent,
  Ere half my days, in this dark world and wide,
  And that one talent which is death to hide
  Lodged with me useless, though my soul more bent
To serve therewith my Maker, and present
  My true account, lest he returning chide,
  'Doth God exact day-labour, light denied?'
  I fondly ask. But Patience, to prevent
That murmur, soon replies: 'God doth not need
  Either man's work or his own gifts; who best
  Bear his mild yoke, they serve him best. His state
Is kingly: thousands at his bidding speed,
  And post o'er land and ocean without rest;
  They also serve who only stand and wait.'

John Milton

Consider the ***rhythm*** *and the* ***rhyme*** *of Milton's sonnet on his blindness, and see how close to the formula of a sonnet the poet has come.* *(See page 80.)* *There are other sonnets in the book on pages 59 and 122.*

✜ *Write your own sonnet – the details of construction are more complicated than those of many verse forms.*

The Fog

I saw the fog grow thick
   Which soon made blind my ken;
It made tall men of boys,
   And giants of tall men.

It clutched my throat, I coughed;
   Nothing was in my head
Except two heavy eyes
   Like balls of burning lead.

And when it grew so black
   That I could know no place,
I lost all judgement then
   Of distance and of space.

The street lamps, and the lights
   Upon the halted cars,
Could either be on earth
   Or be the heavenly stars.

A man passed by me close,
   I asked my way, he said,
'Come, follow me, my friend' –
   I followed where he led.

He walked the stones in front,
   'Trust me,' he said, 'and come':
I followed like a child –
   A blind man led me home.

W. H. Davies

The writer H. G. Wells wrote a short story called ***The Country of the Blind****, based on the saying, 'In the country of the blind the one-eyed man is king.' Wells' story shows that this is not true.*

In ***The Fog*** *the poet W. H. Davies also challenges the idea that the sighted person has the advantage. He uses the imagery of fog to reinforce a distortion of figures which can also occur in darkness or bright sunlight. While these distortions can make the sighted feel as helpless as if they were blind, the blind remain unaffected by them.*

✤ *Write your own poem on the distortions of objects in these conditions; or consider how different sounds might be interpreted by a blind person.*

GERDA MAYER

Gerda Mayer was born in Karlsbad, Czechoslovakia, in 1927, and came to England in 1939, one day before the Germans invaded. She was educated in schools in Dorset and Surrey and at Bedford College, University of London.

Gerda Mayer writes 'I've "written" poems while out walking or while lying in bed. Occasionally, I've had to keep getting out of bed because a poem would occur to me in bits and pieces. Sometimes, a poem gets written while I sit alone in the early hours in my kitchen. Some poems arise in the mind in seconds and virtually complete. Conversely, I've had to wait a decade before getting one four-liner right. The poem always starts in the head. I never sit in front of a piece of blank paper waiting for inspiration.'

Tony Douglas was the Best

In the local Ladies
skinny-legged graffiti
hopscotch their message
of boyfriends and raspberries

One four-letter word
sex turned out as SIX
also HELL'S ANGELS
and COPPERS ARE ROTTEN

But over and above
inside and outside
written tall written small
the name TONY DOUGLAS

That Tony Douglas
I know him well
I've loved him white-haired
I've loved him newly satchelled

Blue-eyed brown-eyed
short tall meagre fat
Tony Douglas was the best
at four at forty

Loved for half an hour
loved for one whole year
under different names
nameless once or twice

Never twice the same
except in one respect
HE OUTSHONE ALL OTHERS
HE OUTSHONE ALL OTHERS

GERDA MAYER

Make Believe

Say I were not sixty,
say you weren't near-hundred,
say you were alive.
Say my verse was read
in some distant country,
and say you were idly turning the pages:

The blood washed from your shirt,
the tears from your eyes,
the earth from your bones:
neither missing since 1940,
nor dead as reported later
by a friend of a friend of a friend . . .

Quite dapper you stand in that bookshop
and chance upon my clues.

That is why at sixty
when some publisher asks me
for biographical details,
I still carefully give
the year of my birth,
the name of my hometown:

GERDA MAYER born '27, in Karlsbad,
Czechoslovakia . . . write to me, father.

Note: The author's father, Arnold Stein, photographed opposite in first World War uniform, escaped from the German concentration camp in Nisko in 1939, fled to Russian-occupied Lemberg/Lwow, and then disappeared in the summer of 1940. It is thought he may have died in a Russian camp.

'I can't normally write to order but ***Make Believe*** *(written in July 1987) was a subject set by a poetry group which I had joined in the hope that it would get me writing again after a long unproductive period.*

'The poem was written within a week and everybody seems to think well of it except the author who suspects it is merely a prose-poem. Should poems go so very bare? Best to slip on some metaphors, similes, rags of wit; some disguise.'

GERDA MAYER

Postcard in Pen and Ink, 1916

Though the perspective is wrong
The picture has been preserved.
Brotherly feeling kept it, as now
Does filial affection. THREE STORKS
ON A THATCHED BARN. The peaceful scene
Done in much black ink is not unsinister.

Not what the young soldier intended,
Surely, though he sent it from the Front.
Three storks augur hope. (How strange
My father foretold me
So long before I was born.)
It's the gaping caverns
That open into the barn
Portend something darker than birth.
Yet not gloom, but too loaded a nib
Probably placed them there.

Well, little stretcher-bearer, yourself
Long stretched out, though surviving
That first grim war to be ground in a far darker,
Your picture outlived you. '1916'
It says. All of sixty-five years
Is, in its way, a small immortality.

'This poem was long in the making, and even in its present completed form is, I suspect, not all that superior to the little picture it derides. There are some very early jottings (crossed out) on an old envelope postmarked April 1975. There were further drafts in 1979. As I can't do the simplest sum in my head, little subtractions (1916 from 1980; '16 from '81) indicate that the "small immortality" was increasing year by year.'

though the perspective is wrong
the picture's been preserved
by brotherly feeling, now
by filial piety:
3 storks
on a thatched barn.
yet the peaceful scene.
done in much black ink
is not unsinister

not what the young
soldier intended, surely,
though he sent it from the front.
3 storks augur hope. (how strange
he should have foretold me
so long before I was born).
but the gaping
caverns that open into the barn
portend something darker
than birth, [illegible] lack of skill
probably placed them here.

well, little stretcher bearer, yourself
long stretched out, your picture survives you.
1916 it says. sixty three years
is in its way a small immortality.

GERDA MAYER

Babes in the Wood

I. M. Hans & Susí Kraus

There is a well known story
Of two little children who crossed
A dark and dangerous forest
And in that forest were lost.

The crumbs they had strewn for their safety
Were picked up by a bird;
The trees had ears and gathered
Every whispered word.

They came to a hut in a clearing,
The name on the door said *HATE*;
Hate hacked them into pieces
And cooked them in the grate.

O forester, hear our voices!
World, pity our cry!
The forester came to dinner,
The world kept rolling by.

The world said *it's unlikely*
That such things can occur;
(Besides, she feared their rescue
Would leave the brats with her).

Alas for the Happy Ending
Of how the tables were turned;
There was no reversal of fortune –
It was Hansel and Gretel who burned.

*'**Babes in the Wood** was begun on 7th March 1962, published in an early version in* The Poetry Review *in spring 1969, and completed in autumn 1969.*

'This is still one of my own favourites. At one stage I had had to abandon the poem altogether. Later, an item in a newspaper revived the original impetus and provided me with the penultimate stanza. Thinking the poem finished, I submitted it to Derek Parker, the then editor of The Poetry Review. *By the time the poem was published, I had thought of all kinds of revisions but had been too timid to bother him with them. (I tend to be bolder now.)*

'By the time it was published in book-form, I had changed the first line because it had been too reminiscent of Auden's poem about Miss Edith Gee. In that third stanza, "wrath" had been too ambiguous, as "wrath" is so often coupled with the epithet "righteous". As the witch was meant to represent the Nazi regime, "wrath" clearly wouldn't do. I substituted the more satisfactory "hate" but then had to forgo the graphic "broth" of the fourth line of this stanza. A compromise!

'The last word in the poem – "burnt" – was changed by my editor and publisher D. J. Enright when he included the poem in Treble Poets 2. *His grammar being more reliable than mine, I've retained his alteration.'*

They came to a hut in a clearing
the name on the door said ~~*Wrath*~~ HATE
Hate ~~Wrath~~ ~~cut~~ them into pieces hacked
and ~~put them into a broth~~ cooked them in the grate

GERDA MAYER

A Lion, a Wolf and a Fox

Stoatley Rough, Haslemere, 1942–1944

I went to school in a forest where I was taught
By a lion, a wolf and a fox.
How the lion shone! As he paced across the sky
We grew brown-limbed in his warmth and among the green leaves.

The fox was a musician. O cunning magician you lured
A small stream from its course with your *Forellenlied*,
Teaching it Schubert; and made the children's voices
All sound like early morning and auguries for a fine day.

Now the wolf was a poet and somewhat grey and reserved,
Something of a lone wolf – thoughts were his pack;
There was a garden in that forest, walled with climbing roses,
Where we would sit or lie and hear the wolf recite.

And sometimes we would listen, and sometimes the voice
Would turn into sunlight on the wall or into a butterfly
Over the grass. It was the garden of poetry and so
Words would turn into flowers and trees into verse.

This morning I received the grey pelt of a wolf,
And the fox and the lion write they are growing old;
That forest lies many years back, but we were in luck
To pass for a spell through that sunny and musical land.

GERDA MAYER

'This is doubtless a rather idealized picture of the last school I attended, from the age of fifteen to seventeen.

'The poem was prompted by the news of the death of Emmy Wolff who had been the German and French mistress there. She was a wonderful speaker of poetry (as well as something of a secret poet herself) and she really did take us out of doors one fine day. Even if our minds wandered a little in all that fragrance and sunshine it was an experience that transcended most things of the classroom.

'The second line of the third stanza originally read,

"... Something of a lone wolf, as many poets are ..."

It struck me later that the statement was glib – many poets being likewise quite convivial. I replaced "as many poets are" with "thoughts were his pack" – "pack" to be read as his "companions" (i.e. wolf-pack) and also as his "burden".'

GERDA MAYER

The Hansel and Gretel House

When you come across it
you'll know better than to
nibble.
Who's there? asks the witch.
The wind, cry the
startled children.

A house may look sweet
from outside: beware!
Things happen in pretty houses
you wouldn't believe...

When the wind cries,
when the dog weeps,
when the voice of lost children
is heard in the wood,
let the forester hasten forth.

*'There are seventeen years between the writing of the first Hansel and Gretel poem (**Babes in the Wood**) and this one. Here Hansel and Gretel represent children who are ill-treated in our own day. The poem centres on the lines,*

> Things happen in pretty houses/you wouldn't believe.'

The Man on the Desert Island

The man on the desert island
Has forgotten the ways of people,
His stories are all of himself.
Day in, day out of time,
He communes with himself and sends
Messages in green bottles:
Help me they say *I am*
Cast up and far from home.
Each day he goes to watch
The horizon for ships.
Nothing reaches his shore
Except corked green bottles.

Written 15th May 1961, 3.30 am.

'It looks as if this poem had been written fairly quickly in the early hours, on the kitchen table. Our kitchen has a big clock and it is only when I am writing there that I bother to look up and note the exact moment a poem is finished.

'I am still fond of this little poem. It is, of course, about a stubborn, insoluble loneliness. The messages the man on the desert island sends out come floating back to him, unanswered.'

GERDA MAYER

529 1983

Absentmindedly,
sometimes,
I lift the receiver
And dial my own number.

(What revelations,
I think then,
If only
I could get through to myself.)

'I think I wrote this poem fairly quickly on 1st September 1975. Although it is a jocular little poem and intended to amuse, it is really about the difficulty of understanding one's own motives. The "revelations" if one could "get through" to oneself would be self-knowledge.'

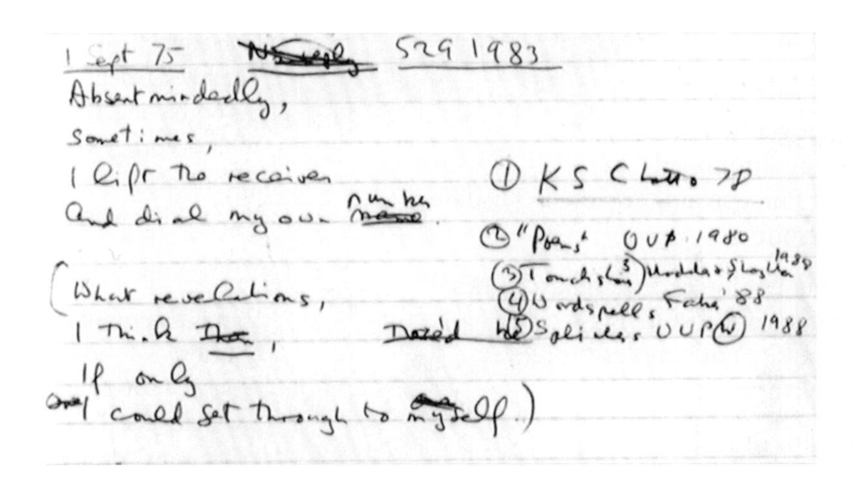

1 Sept 75 ~~[illegible]~~ 529 1983

Absentmindedly,
Sometimes,
I lift the receiver
And dial my own number.

(What revelations,
I think then,
If only
I could get through to myself.)

① K S Chatto 78
② "Poems" OUP 1980
③ Touchstones 3 [illegible] 1980
④ Wordspells, Faber '88
⑤ Spells, OUP [illegible] 1988

GERDA MAYER

The Seven

AVARICE had a bad childhood
And thrift is her problem.
All her clobber's in rags;
She can't spare the thread for the mending.

Once LUST at his best
Was coarsely benevolent:
Now his largesse
Aids we don't know whom.

WRATH rattles the cage of ribs
And bellows for his release.
Deny him too long
And he'll chew up your heart.

PRIDE's a proper gentleman.
How was he ever confounded
With his brother Purseproud, his cousin Disdain,
His servile son Snob?

GLUTTONY, big booby, except in hard times
Why should anyone mind you?
You simply like a lot. Your cholesterol level
Is surely your own affair.

SLOTH, you slattern,
You slippered scandal, you frump,
The other housewives make beds, jams, doilies.
(Amazing how careworn their faces.)

You envy them all, ENVY.
You've told me again and again
That whatever they say to the contrary
You are the worst off.

'This poem was written in October 1980. However, the idea of writing indulgently about the Seven Deadly Sins came from a New Statesman Weekend *competition five years earlier.*

'Lust was re-written for my Peterloo Poets collection A Heartache of Grass, *1988. There are two versions of* **Envy** *and I think I now favour the one in* New Poetry 9, *published in 1983:*

You envy them all, ENVY:
Their zest, their wealth, their
  good living, their ease.
Whatever they say to the
  contrary,
You are the worst off.

'I give below two earlier attempts:

Lust is free of inhibitions,
Gluttony knows how to dine,
Avarice is thrift and forethought,
Social justice, Envy's whine.
Pride is proper, righteous Wrath is,
But the sweetest cheerful Sloth is.

Pride shushed Avarice,
Avarice chid Gluttony,
Gluttony harried Sloth:
(Bring me my pudding).
Sloth held up Anger,
Anger beat Envy,
Envy toppled Pride.
Lust died.

'In the latter, the Sins exercise a restraining influence on each other.'

GERDA MAYER

Tony Douglas
Collect some graffiti. Write a poem around it.

Make Believe
How much autobiographical information is in the poem? What would you like undone in your past? Who would you most like to see again? What details would you pick for your autobiographical poem?

Postcard
Has anyone kept a picture you drew when you were very small? Imagine one of your children years in the future looking at it and writing about you.

Hansel and Gretel
Choose a fairy tale to retell: ***Cinderella*** *from the point of view of one of the 'ugly' sisters, or* ***Little Red Riding Hood*** *as a story about talking to strangers.*

A Lion, a Wolf and a Fox
What animals are your teachers? What animal are you?

Man on a Desert Island
The message in a bottle is rather like graffiti: a cry into the unknown. A modern equivalent would be beaming a radio message into space. What would you send?

529 1983
What would you hear if you could get through to yourself?

The Seven
What would be your seven deadly sins, the worst things people can do?

Wrath
A good model to imitate. Treat the feeling as if it was an animal. What kind? How would it behave?

Seeing Granny

Toothless, she kisses
with fleshly lips
rounded, like mouth
of a bottle, all wet.

She bruises your face
almost, with two
loving tree-root hands.

She makes you sit, fixed.
She then stuffs you
with boiled pudding and lemonade.

She watches you feed
on her food. She milks
you dry of answers
about the goat she gave you.

James Berry

Everyone is likely to meet old age – in friends, in relations, in everyday life. These two poems, ***Seeing Granny*** *and* ***Old Age Report****, express the poets' inward feelings towards particular old people.*

Consider what features make people seem old, e.g. behaviour, movement. Discuss what else makes people appear old.

✥ *Write a poem expressing your inward and outward feelings towards an old or handicapped person.*

Old Age Report

When a man's too ill or old to work
We punish him.
Half his income is taken away
Or all of it vanishes and he gets pocket-money.

We should reward these tough old humans for surviving.
Not with a manager's soggy handshake
Or a medal shaped like an alarm clock –
No, make them a bit rich,
Give the freedom they always heard about
When the bloody chips were down
And the blitz or the desert
Swallowed their friends.

Retire, retire into a fungus basement
Where nothing moves except the draught
And the light and dark grey figures
Doubling their money on the screen;
Where the cabbages taste like the mummy's hand
And the meat tastes of feet;
Where there is nothing to say except:
'Remember?' or 'Your turn to dust the cat.'

To hell with retiring. Let them advance.
Give them the money they've always earned
Or more – and let them choose.
If Mr Burley wants to be a miser,
Great, let the moneybags sway and clink for him.
Pay him a pillowful of best doubloons.
So Mrs Wells has always longed to travel?
Print her a season ticket to the universe.
Let her slum-white skin
Be tanned by a dozen different planets.
We could wipe away some of their worry,
Some of their pain – what I mean
Is so bloody simple:
The old people are being robbed
And punished and we ought
To be letting them out of their cages
Into green spaces of enchanting light.

Adrian Mitchell

The next two poems consider the approach of death.

Do not go Gentle into that Good Night

Do not go gentle into that good night.
Old age should burn and rave at close of day;
Rage, rage against the dying of the light.

Though wise men at their end know dark is right,
Because their words had forked no lightning they
Do not go gentle into that good night.

Good men, the last wave by, crying how bright
Their frail deeds might have danced in a green bay,
Rage, rage against the dying of the light.

Wild men who caught and sang the sun in flight,
And learn, too late, they grieved it on its way,
Do not go gentle into that good night.

Grave men, near death, who see with blinding sight
Blind eyes could blaze like meteors and be gay,
Rage, rage against the dying of the light.

And you, my father, there on the sad height,
Curse, bless, me now with your fierce tears, I pray.
Do not go gentle into that good night.
Rage, rage against the dying of the light.

Dylan Thomas

Dylan Thomas wrote this elegy for his dying father in 1951. (An elegy is a formal lament for the death of a particular person.) It is in the form of a **villanelle**. *(See page 80 on* **verse forms**.*)*

✤ *Look carefully at the regularity of this structure, then compose a similar piece, perhaps for a dying woman, a relation or a friend.*

'A good poem is a contribution to reality. The world is never the same once a good poem has been added to it.'
Dylan Thomas

Conscientious Objector

I shall die, but that is all that I shall do for Death.

I hear him leading his horse out of the stall; I hear the
  clatter on the barn-floor.
He is in haste; he has business in Cuba, business in the
  Balkans, many calls to make this morning.
But I will not hold the bridle while he cinches the girth.
And he may mount by himself; I will not give him a leg
  up.

Though he flick my shoulders with his whip, I will not
  tell him which way the fox ran.
With his hoof on my breast, I will not tell him where the
  black boy hides in the swamp.
I shall die, but that is all that I shall do for Death; I am
  not on his pay-roll.

I will not tell him the whereabouts of my friends nor of
  my enemies either.
Though he promise me much, I will not map him the
  route to any man's door.

Am I a spy in the land of the living, that I should deliver
  men to Death?
Brother, the password and the plans of our city are safe
  with me; never through me
Shall you be overcome.

Edna St Vincent Millay

Conscientious Objector *shows a personification of death (see* ***image*** *on page 36). Death is often represented as a person, e.g. the grim reaper with a scythe.*

✤ *Consider a new, modern image for death and write your own poem about meeting – or cheating? – death.*

Ozymandias

I met a traveller from an antique land
Who said: Two vast and trunkless legs of stone
Stand in the desert. Near them on the sand,
Half sunk, a shatter'd visage lies, whose frown
And wrinkled lip and sneer of cold command
Tell that its sculptor well those passions read
Which yet survive, stamp'd on these lifeless things,
The hand that mock'd them and the heart that fed;
And on the pedestal these words appear:
'My name is Ozymandias, king of kings:
Look on my works, ye Mighty, and despair!'
Nothing beside remains. Round the decay
Of that colossal wreck, boundless and bare,
The lone and level sands stretch far away.

Percy Bysshe Shelley

[Fragment of an earlier draft]

There stands by Nile a single pedestal,
On which two trunkless legs of crumbling stone
Quiver through sultry mist; beneath the sand
Half sunk a shattered visage lies, whose frown
And wrinkled lips impatient of command
Betray some sculptor's art, who

The fragment of the earlier draft of ***Ozymandias*** *shown here reveals that Shelley made many changes to the early lines of this well-known poem, another example of the* ***sonnet*** *(see page 80).*

It started as a description

There stands . . .

but becomes a report from a traveller: what is the effect of this change?

Two trunkless legs of crumbling stone

has become

two vast and trunkless legs of stone

Which is better and why?

Quiver through sultry mist

becomes

stand in the desert

The second is simpler, but is it better?

Are there other changes which make the language simpler?

✤ *Write your own sonnet about a present day object that might be discovered in the future, showing the brief span of people's lives and of their creations.*

> *'Poetry is the record of the best and happiest moments of the happiest and best minds.'*
>
> *Percy Bysshe Shelley*

My name is Ozymandias – King of Kings

with a lone single pedestal,

which, Two trunkless legs are crumbling

The wreck of a colossal form

Two trunkless legs of

beneath the sand

half sunk whose gathered frown

wrinkled lip impatient of command

Whose gathered frown, & curved lips

Half sunk a shattered visage

Cannot we rest until

Relic

I found this jawbone at the sea's edge:
There, crabs, dogfish, broken by the breakers or tossed
To flap for half an hour and turn to a crust
Continue the beginning. The deeps are cold:
In that darkness camaraderie does not hold:
Nothing touches but, clutching, devours. And the jaws,
Before they are satisfied or their stretched purpose
Slacken, go down jaws; go gnawn bare. Jaws
Eat and are finished and the jawbone comes to the beach:
This is the sea's achievement; with shells,
Vertebrae, claws, carapaces, skulls.

Time in the sea eats its tail, thrives, casts these
Indigestibles, the spars of purposes
That failed far from the surface. None grow rich
In the sea. This curved jawbone did not laugh
But gripped, gripped and is now a cenotaph.

Ted Hughes

Relic *also describes an old object which is discovered and brings to mind its age, its history and its end, in the same way as* ***Ozymandias*** *does with a statue.*

'The one thing is, imagine what you are writing about. See it and live it.'
Ted Hughes

The River God

I may be smelly and I may be old,
Rough in my pebbles, reedy in my pools,
But where my fish float by I bless their swimming
And I like the people to bathe in me, especially women.
But I can drown the fools
Who bathe too close to the weir, contrary to rules.
And they take a long time drowning
As I throw them up now and then in a spirit of clowning.
Hi yih, yippity-yap, merrily I flow,
Oh I may be an old foul river but I have plenty of go.
Once there was a lady who was too bold
She bathed in me by the tall black cliff where the water
   runs cold,
So I brought her down here
To be my beautiful dear.
Oh will she stay with me will she stay
This beautiful lady, or will she go away?
She lies in my beautiful deep river bed with many a
   weed
To hold her, and many a waving reed.
Oh who would guess what a beautiful white face lies
   there
Waiting for me to smooth and wash away the fear
She looks at me with. Hi yih, do not let her
Go. There is no one on earth who does not forget her
Now. They say I am a foolish old smelly river
But they do not know of my wide original bed
Where the lady waits, with her golden sleepy head.
If she wishes to go I will not forgive her.

Stevie Smith

***The River God** shows a personification of a river. This is another example of **extended metaphor**. Many people in the ancient world believed that woods, rivers and mountains were inhabited by spirits.*

✤ *Try writing your own poem giving a personality to some everyday object which is reflecting on its experieces, e.g. a bus, a tube train, a settee, a bath.*

The next four poems are reflections on the purpose and meaning of life.

I Stood on a Tower in the Wet

I stood on a tower in the wet,
And New Year and Old Year met,
And winds were roaring and blowing;
And I said, 'O years, that meet in tears,
Have ye aught that is worth the knowing?
Science enough and exploring,
Wanderers coming and going,
Matter enough for deploring,
But aught that is worth the knowing?'
Seas at my feet were flowing,
Waves on the shingle pouring,
Old Year roaring and blowing,
And New Year blowing and roaring.

Alfred, Lord Tennyson

✤ *The arrival of the New Year is often a time to reconsider first principles, as Tennyson does. Write your own poem, and try to imitate the repetition so obvious in this poem.*

Days

What are days for?
Days are where we live.
They come, they wake us
Time and time over.
They are to be happy in:
Where can we live but days?

Ah, solving that question
Brings the priest and the doctor
In their long coats
Running over the fields.

Philip Larkin

*Are there other answers and other solutions to the questions in **Days**?*

who knows if the moon's

who knows if the moon's
a balloon, coming out of a keen city
in the sky – filled with pretty people?
(and if you and i should

get into it, if they
should take me and take you into their balloon,
why then
we'd go up higher with all the pretty people

than houses and steeples and clouds:
go sailing
away and away sailing into a keen
city which nobody's ever visited, where

always
          it's
                    Spring) and everyone's
in love and flowers pick themselves

e. e. cummings

e. e. cummings is known for his unconventional style – no capitals (even in his name!). Discuss what other unconventional features you notice about his style.

✣ *Try a* **pastiche** *of this style, describing a fantasy journey of your own.*

I Stepped from Plank to Plank

I stepped from plank to plank,
A slow and cautious way;
The stars about my head I felt,
About my feet the sea.

I knew not but the next
Would be my final inch.
This gave me that precarious gait
Some call experience.

Emily Dickinson

✣ *Try a* **pastiche** *of Emily Dickinson's poem, using a modern image for the journey of life.*

'If . . . it makes my whole body so cold no fire can warm me, I know that is poetry.'
Emily Dickinson

Leisure

What is this life if, full of care,
We have no time to stand and stare?

No time to stand beneath the boughs
And stare as long as sheep or cows;

No time to see, when woods we pass,
Where squirrels hide their nuts in grass;

No time to see, in broad daylight,
Streams full of stars, like skies at night;

No time to turn at Beauty's glance,
And watch her feet, how they can dance;

No time to wait till her mouth can
Enrich that smile her eyes began?

A poor life this if, full of care,
We have no time to stand and stare.

W. H. Davies

The couplets in W. H. Davies' ***Leisure*** *are reminiscent of Blake (see page 15). Discuss what you feel is rewarding to 'stand and stare' at nowadays.*

✤ *Compose a group poem: use the same opening couplet as Davies and then let each member of the group contribute a couplet.*

The Pessimist

Nothing to do but work,
  Nothing to eat but food,
Nothing to wear but clothes,
  To keep one from going nude.

Nothing to breathe but air,
  Quick as a flash 'tis gone;
Nowhere to fall but off,
  Nowhere to stand but on.

Nothing to comb but hair,
  Nowhere to sleep but in bed,
Nothing to weep but tears,
  Nothing to bury but dead.

Nothing to sing but songs,
  Ah, well, alas! alack!
Nowhere to go but out,
  Nowhere to come but back.

Nothing to see but sights,
  Nothing to quench but thirst,
Nothing to have but what we've got.
  Thus thro' life we are cursed.

Nothing to strike but a gait;
  Everything moves that goes.
Nothing at all but common sense
  Can ever withstand these woes.

Benjamin Franklin King

***The Pessimist** uses regular rhythm and rhyme and obvious repetition for its effect.*

✤ *Write your own **pastiche** of this. You could choose a similar theme of pessimism, with repeated negatives, or a poem called **The Optimist**, also using repetition.*

Many pupils at school have views on what they would prefer to be studying. These two poems by Whitman and Causley consider that. Read them and compare them with Gerda Mayer's poem about her teachers (page 110).

When I Heard the Learn'd Astronomer

When I heard the learn'd astronomer,
When the proofs, the figures, were ranged in columns before me,
When I was shown the charts and diagrams, to add, divide, and measure them,
When I sitting heard the astronomer where he lectured with much applause in the lecture-room,
How soon unaccountable I became tired and sick,
Till rising and gliding out I wander'd off by myself,
In the mystical moist night-air, and from time to time,
Look'd up in perfect silence at the stars.

Walt Whitman

> *'To have great poets there must be great audiences too.'*
>
> *Walt Whitman*

School at Four O'clock

At four o'clock the building enters harbour.
All day it seems that we have been at sea.
Now, having lurched through the last of the water,
We lie, stone-safe, beside the jumping quay.
The stiff waves propped against the classroom window,
The razor-back of cliffs we never pass,
The question-mark of green coiling behind us,
Have all turned into cabbages, slates, grass.

Up the slow hill a squabble of children wanders
As silence dries the valley like a drought,
When suddenly that speechless cry is raging
Once more round these four walls to be let out.
Like playing cards the Delabole slates flutter,
The founding stone is shaken in its mine,
The faultless evening light begins to stutter
As the cry hurtles down the chimney-spine.

Packing my bag with useless bits of paper
I wonder, when the last word has been said,
If I'd prefer to find each sound was thudding
Not round the school, but just inside my head.
I watch where the street lamp with sodium finger
Touches the darkening voices as they fall.
Outside? Inside? Perhaps either condition's
Better than his who hears nothing at all.

And I recall another voice. A teacher
Long years ago, saying, *I think I know*
Where all the children come from, but the puzzle
To me is, as they grow up, where they go?
Love, wonder, marvellous hope. All these can wither
With crawling years like flowers on a stalk;
Or, to some Piper's tune, vanish for ever
As creatures murdered on a morning walk.

Though men may blow this building up with powder,
Drag its stone guts to knacker's yard, or tip,
Smash its huge heart to dust, and spread the shingle
By the strong sea, or sink it like a ship –
Listen. Through the clear shell of air the voices
Still strike like water from the mountain bed;
The cry of those who to a certain valley
Hungry and innocent came. And were not fed.

Charles Causley

✤ *Write your own poem about the ideal programme for school. Choose a verse form to imitate from those you have met.*

A Martian Sends a Postcard Home

Caxtons are mechanical birds with many wings
and some are treasured for their markings –

they cause the eyes to melt
or the body to shriek without pain.

I have never seen one fly, but
sometimes they perch on the hand.

Mist is when the sky is tired of flight
and rests its soft machine on ground:

then the world is dim and bookish
like engravings under tissue paper.

Rain is when the earth is television.
It has the property of making colours darker.

Model T is a room with the lock inside –
a key is turned to free the world

for movement, so quick there is a film
to watch for anything missed.

But time is tied to the wrist
or kept in a box, ticking with impatience.

In homes, a haunted apparatus sleeps,
that snores when you pick it up.

If the ghost cries, they carry it
to their lips and soothe it to sleep

with sounds. And yet, they wake it up
deliberately, by tickling with a finger.

Only the young are allowed to suffer
openly. Adults go to a punishment room

with water but nothing to eat.
They lock the door and suffer the noises

alone. No one is exempt
and everyone's pain has a different smell.

At night, when all the colours die,
they hide in pairs

and read about themselves –
in colour, with their eyelids shut.

Craig Raine

The Martian's postcard contains many novel ***images*** *for everyday objects and events. Discuss the various* ***metaphors*** *and discover what all the objects are, to which Craig Raine refers.*

✤ *Write some more postcards of your own, with couplets for different metaphors; or compile a 'group postcard', with each member contributing one metaphor as a couplet.*

✤ *The unusual views of a visitor to Earth lead to a journey into space from Earth, in* ***The First Journey****. Write a story poem of a journey from a destroyed Earth to a new planet. Follow the same pattern of stanzas, starting with:*

Once upon . . .

On the . . .

On the . . .

The First Journey

Once upon a time
Beyond the outer universe
On the far black meadows of nowhere
The human race assembled.
We made sure everyone was present and prepared.
Then we began our journey.

Under Niagaras of meteorites
Through jungle galaxies,
Over deserts of ammonia,
Along the million-year-deep canyons
Which gape between the stars,
We travelled together,
Towards the light,
Looking for a home.

On the planet Pluto
And on the planet Neptune
And on the planet Uranus
We froze in chemical oceans.
The sun no brighter than a match.

On the planet Saturn
The triple rings of silver
Dazzled and maddened us.

On the planet Jupiter
We were apples in the cider press
Of massive gravity.

On the planet Mars
We cried with thirst
And our tears were yellow dust.

On the planet Venus
We suffocated
Under four hundred miles
Of soaking clouds.

On the planet Mercury
We were offered
A choice of death by heat or cold.

But then we saw her
We saw our planet
Our earth
Our home

Let the people of the world
Shake off their chains and sing

There is no heaven but the Earth
There is no heaven but the People

Let the people of the world
Shake off their chains
And dance
And dance towards the light
Towards whatever shines.

Song in Space

When man first flew beyond the sky
He looked back into the world's blue eye.
Man said: What makes your eye so blue?
Earth said: The tears in the oceans do.
Why are the seas so full of tears?
Because I've wept so many thousand years.
Why do you weep as you dance through space?
Because I am the mother of the human race.

Adrian Mitchell

U. A. FANTHORPE

'I began writing poetry out of self-defence. I had taken on a job as hospital receptionist which was very different from my previous job (teaching English). Instead of being in charge of things, more or less, I suddenly found myself at the beck and call of patients, nurses and doctors, none of whom wanted to listen to what I had to say or to my brilliant ideas for improving the system. After a month of hard and angry thinking and feeling, and of not being listened to at all, I broke out into poetry. Having broken out, I found I felt infinitely better. To write is to heal oneself: this is the most important thing I can tell you. Nowadays I write for other reasons as well: to find out the answers to puzzles, to bring to life a word or image that haunts me, or simply because an idea or image becomes importunate – just as, in the First World War, people sometimes said that a bullet had their name on it, so sometimes an unwritten poem has my name on it.

'How do I write? I discovered a good method by accident. At the hospital, my lunch-hour was forty minutes, and I could spend it alone in a caravan that was full of scrap paper. The basic needs for a poet are pen or pencil, and paper. You don't need too much time, because writing poetry is very demanding, and about twenty minutes' worth is all I can do in a session. The remaining twenty minutes goes on revision. I find I can write almost anywhere (e.g., on a bus, sitting on a wall, etc.) but not at a desk. Two vital aids: Roget's *Thesaurus*, and a really good dictionary.'

Dear Mr Lee

Dear Mr Lee (Mr Smart says
it's rude to call you Laurie, but that's
how I think of you, having lived with you
really all year), Dear Mr Lee
(Laurie) I just want you to know
I used to hate English, and Mr Smart
is roughly my least favourite person,
and as for Shakespeare (we're doing him too)
I think he's a national disaster, with all those jokes
that Mr Smart has to explain why they're jokes,
and even then no one thinks they're funny,
And T. Hughes and P. Larkin and that lot
in our anthology, not exactly a laugh a minute,
pretty gloomy really, so that's why
I wanted to say Dear Laurie (sorry) your book's
the one that made up for the others, if you

could see my copy you'd know it's lived
with me, stained with Coke and Kitkat
and when I had a cold, and I often
take you to bed with me to cheer me up
so Dear Laurie, I want to say sorry,
I didn't want to write a character-sketch
of your mother under headings, it seemed
wrong somehow when you'd made her so lovely,
and I didn't much like those questions
about *social welfare in the rural community*
and *the seasons as perceived by an adolescent*,
I didn't think you'd want your book
read that way, but bits of it I know by heart,
and I wish I had your uncles and your half-sisters
and lived in Slad, though Mr Smart says your view
of the class struggle is naïve, and the examiners
won't be impressed by me knowing so much by heart,
they'll be looking for terse and cogent answers
to their questions, but I'm not much good at terse and cogent,
I'd just like to be like you, not mind about being poor,
see everything bright and strange, the way you do,
and I've got the next one out of the Public Library,
about Spain, and I asked Mum about learning
to play the fiddle, but Mr Smart says Spain isn't
like that any more, it's all Timeshare villas
and Torremolinos, and how old were you
when you became a poet? (Mr Smart says for anyone
with my punctuation to consider poetry as a career
is enough to make the angels weep).

PS Dear Laurie, please don't feel guilty
for me failing the exam, it wasn't your
fault, it was mine, and Shakespeare's,
and maybe Mr Smart's, I still love *Cider*,
it hasn't made any difference.

'I was asked to write this for a celebration in honour of the Gloucestershire writer Laurie Lee. It was hard to do, so I turned it into a letter from someone who has had to study ***Cider With Rosie*** *for an exam.*

U. A. FANTHORPE

Knowing about Sonnets

Lesson 1: 'The Soldier' (Brooke)

'(The task of criticism) is not to redouble the text's self-understanding, to collude with its object in a conspiracy of silence. The task is to show the text as it cannot know itself.'
(Terry Eagleton: Criticism and Ideology)

Recognising a sonnet is like attaching
A name to a face. *Mister Sonnet, I presume?*
    If I
And naming is power. It can hardly
Deny its name. You are well on the way
To mastery. The next step is telling the sonnet
What it is trying to say. This is called Interpretation.
    If I should die
What you mustn't do is collude with it. This
Is bad for the sonnet, and will only encourage it
To be eloquent. You must question it closely:
What has it left out? What made it decide
To be a sonnet? The author's testimony
(If any) is not evidence. He is the last person to know.
    If I should die, think this
Stand no nonsense with imagery. Remember, though shifty,
It is vulnerable to calculation. Apply the right tests.
Now you are able to Evaluate the sonnet.
    If I
That should do for today.
    If I should die
                And over and over
The new white paper track innocent unlined hands.
    Think this. Think this. Think this. Think only this.

'I wrote this after listening to a university lecture in which the lecturer approved of Mr Eagleton and didn't really like Rupert Brooke's sonnet. I wanted to give Rupert Brooke a chance to answer back, because he was talking, in however sentimental a way, about something very hard: the moment when a young man realizes that he's going to die, and it may be soon. All that Brooke says is from his poem, and he says it very quietly and hesitantly, and the important word for him is "die". The lecturer says a lot. Would you say he likes poetry? The last line belongs to both Brooke and the lecturer, in turn.'

U. A. FANTHORPE

Patience Strong

'This is a true story from my hospital days. For about fifty years Patience Strong wrote short uplifting rhymes in women's magazines and on calendars, which are mysteriously not arranged as rhyme. You will realize that all poets are jealous of her, though they don't care to admit it. You might be interested in my reasons for talking about Patience Strong before telling the story.'

Everyone knows her name. Trite calendars
Of rose-nooked cottages or winding ways
Display her sentiments in homespun verse
Disguised as prose. She has her tiny niche
In women's magazines, too, tucked away
Among the recipes or near the end
Of some perennial serial. Her theme
Always the same: rain falls in every life,
But rainbows, bluebirds, spring, babies or God
Lift up our hearts. No doubt such rubbish sells.
She must be feathering her inglenook.
Genuine poets seldom coin the stuff,
Nor do they flaunt such aptly bogus names.
Their message is oblique; it doesn't fit
A pocket diary's page; nor does it pay.

One day in epileptic out-patients,
A working-man, a fellow in his fifties,
Was feeling bad. I brought a cup of tea.
He talked about his family and job:
His dad was in the Ambulance Brigade;
He hoped to join, but being epileptic,
They wouldn't have him. *Naturally*, he said,
With my disease, I'd be a handicap.
But I'd have liked to help. He sucked his tea,
Then from some special inner pocket brought
A booklet muffled up in cellophane,
Unwrapped it gently, opened at a page –
Characteristic cottage garden, seen
Through chintzy casement windows. Underneath
Some cosy musing in the usual vein,
And *See*, he said, *this is what keeps me going*.

U. A. FANTHORPE

Not my Best Side

I

Not my best side, I'm afraid.
The artist didn't give me a chance to
Pose properly, and as you can see,
Poor chap, he had this obsession with
Triangles, so he left off two of my
Feet. I didn't comment at the time
(What, after all, are two feet
To a monster?) but afterwards
I was sorry for the bad publicity.
Why, I said to myself, should my conqueror
Be so ostentatiously beardless, and ride
A horse with a deformed neck and square hoofs?
Why should my victim be so
Unattractive as to be inedible,
And why should she have me literally
On a string? I don't mind dying
Ritually, since I always rise again,
But I should have liked a little more blood
To show they were taking me seriously.

II

It's hard for a girl to be sure if
She wants to be rescued. I mean, I quite
Took to the dragon. It's nice to be
Liked, if you know what I mean. He was
So nicely physical, with his claws
And lovely green skin, and that sexy tail,
And the way he looked at me,
He made me feel he was all ready to
Eat me. And any girl enjoys that.
So when this boy turned up, wearing machinery,
On a really *dangerous* horse, to be honest,
I didn't much fancy him. I mean,
What was he like underneath the hardware?
He might have acne, blackheads or even
Bad breath for all I could tell, but the dragon –
Well, you could see all his equipment
At a glance. Still, what could I do?
The dragon got himself beaten by the boy,
And a girl's got to think of her future.

III

I have diplomas in Dragon
Management and Virgin Reclamation.
My horse is the latest model, with
Automatic transmission and built-in
Obsolescence. My spear is custom-built,
And my prototype armour
Still on the secret list. You can't
Do better than me at the moment.
I'm qualified and equipped to the
Eyebrow. So why be difficult?
Don't you want to be killed and/or rescued
In the most contemporary way? Don't
You want to carry out the roles
That sociology and myth have designed for you?
Don't you realise that, by being choosy,
You are endangering job-prospects
In the spear- and horse-building industries?
What, in any case, does it matter what
You want? You're in my way.

'This is based on Uccello's painting of St George and the Dragon, which you can see in the National Gallery in London. I thought it might be interesting to find voices for characters who are usually seen as conventionally good, bad, or helpless.'

U. A. FANTHORPE

Swifts

Inland birds are earthbound;
Potter on lawns, squat obstinately
On hot tarmac, loiter under hedges,
Shuffle pigeon-toed along piazzas,
Hang desperate and upside-down on bacon rind,
Pose like debutantes against suitable landscapes –
Anything to avoid the bother of flying.

Only these immigrants are aeronauts,
Spinning their circuits in untroubled air.
Black as magicians, bird's eye view of birds,
A straight line and a curve is all they are.

Their idle ambits trap the invisible
Invisibly. Dark dolphins of the sky,
They mate and eat in their bright element,
And never turn to earth until they die.

'I wrote this because (as you might guess) I like swifts. To establish their strangeness, it seemed necessary to write first about resident birds, and describe them as if they were people. This underlines the black agile otherness of swifts.'

Swifts

Inland birds are earthbound.
They potter on lawns, squat obstinately
On hot tarmac, loiter ~~along~~ hedgerows,
Shuffle pigeon-toed ~~round~~ piazzas,
Hang desperate and upside-down on bacon rind,
Pose like debutantes against suitable landscapes
-- Anything to avoid the bother of flying.

Only these immigrants are aeronauts,
Spinning their circuits in untroubled air.

Black as magicians, bird's eye view of bird,
A straight line and a curve is all they are.

Their idle ambits trap the invisible
Invisibly. Dark dolphins of the sky,

They ~~meet~~ mate and feed in their bright element;
~~Earth never catches~~ them until they die.
And never falls to earth until they die.

U. A. FANTHORPE

Children Imagining a Hospital

For Kingswood County Primary School

'I was asked to write this poem as a contribution to the Wishing Well Appeal for Great Ormond Street Children's Hospital. The best way to handle this seemed to be to ask real children to imagine what a good hospital would be like. They didn't think much about being ill, you'll notice.'

I would like kindness, assurance,
A wide selection of books;
Lots of visitors, and a friend
To come and see me:
A bed by the window so I could look at
All the trees and fields, where I could go for a walk.
I'd like a hospital with popcorn to eat.
A place where I have my own way.

I would like HTV all to myself
And people bringing tea round on trollies;
Plenty of presents and plenty of cards
(I would like presents of food).
Things on the walls, like pictures, and things
That hang from the ceiling;
Long corridors to whizz down in wheelchairs.
Not to be left alone.

Our Dog Chasing Swifts

A border collie has been bred to keep
Order among those wayward bleaters, sheep.
Ours, in a sheepless garden, vainly tries
To herd the screaming black sheep of the skies.

'I was asked by Michael Harrison to write some four-liners, a thing which I found fun to do, as you might. It seemed necessary, in such a very short poem, to tie it together with rhyme.'

Reindeer Report

Chimneys: colder.
Flightpaths: busier.
Driver: Christmas (F)
Still baffled by postcodes.

Children: more
And stay up later.
Presents: heavier.
Pay: frozen.

Mission in spite
Of all this
Accomplished:

'This was written to be printed at home on a hand press at Christmas. It was therefore important to be as brief as possible, since hand-setting type is difficult. This is why I have used the formula noun: adjective *as much as I could, for economy. I've also tried to make it as up-to-date as possible.'*

BC:AD

This was the moment when Before
Turned into After, and the future's
Uninvented timekeepers presented arms.

This was the moment when nothing
Happened. Only dull peace
Sprawled boringly over the earth.

This was the moment when even energetic Romans
Could find nothing better to do
Than counting heads in remote provinces.

And this was the moment
When a few farm workers and three
Members of an obscure Persian sect

Walked haphazard by starlight straight
Into the kingdom of heaven.

'Another Christmas poem written for the press at home. Each year's subject has to be different, which is hard, since the material is essentially always the same. As you'll see, I've avoided the usual words "shepherds" and "wise men"; I did have a reason for this.'

U. A. FANTHORPE

You will be Hearing from us Shortly

You feel adequate to the demands of this position?
What qualities do you feel you
Personally have to offer?

Ah

Let us consider your application form.
Your qualifications, though impressive, are
Not, we must admit, precisely what
We had in mind. Would you care
To defend their relevance?

Indeed

Now your age. Perhaps you feel able
To make your own comment about that,
Too? We are conscious ourselves
Of the need for a candidate with precisely
The right degree of immaturity.

So glad we agree

And now a delicate matter: your looks.
You do appreciate this work involves
Contact with the actual public? Might they,
Perhaps, find your appearance
Disturbing?

Quite so

And your accent. That is the way
You have always spoken, is it? What
Of your education? Were
You educated? We mean, of course,
Where were you educated?

And how

Much of a handicap is that to you,
Would you say?

Married, children,

We see. The usual dubious
Desire to perpetuate what had better
Not have happened at all. We do not
Ask what domestic disasters shimmer
Behind that vaguely unsuitable address.
And you were born – ?

Yes. Pity.

So glad we agree.

'This really needs to be read aloud. It is written for a chorus of interviewers and one silent candidate. The reason for this is that candidates naturally say very different things, but whatever they say is wrong. There was therefore no need to write that part in; but it is important to leave a gap between the questions for the (silent) response.'

✣ *Write a poem about a picture.*
Try a rhyming four-liner.
Write a poem about someone you dislike, but at the same time in some way admire.
Write a letter-poem to the author of a book you don't like.
Imagine yourself to be someone who has a very bad reputation (like Hitler) and write a poem to justify yourself, perhaps without seeing the need to justify yourself.
Write a poem about a dramatic event, set in your garden, with no human beings involved.

Where do poets' ideas come from? There now follows a selection of poems that have arisen from various stimuli: buildings, sculpture, tombs, paintings, dreams. We have included illustrations or descriptions of these stimuli.

Anne Frank Huis

Even now, after twice her lifetime of grief
and anger in the very place, whoever comes
to climb these narrow stairs, discovers how
the bookcase slides aside, then walks through
shadow into sunlit rooms, can never help

but break her secrecy again. Just listening
is a kind of guilt: the Westerkerk repeats
itself outside, as if all time worked round
towards her fear, and made each stroke die
down on guarded streets. Imagine it

three years of whispering and loneliness
and plotting, day by day, the Allied line
in Europe with a yellow chalk. What hope
she had for ordinary love and interest
survives her here, displayed above the bed

as pictures of her family; some actors;
fashions chosen by Princess Elizabeth.
And those who stoop to see them find
not only patience missing its reward,
but one enduring wish for chances like

my own: to leave as simply as I do,
and walk where couples stroll at ease
up dusty tree-lined avenues, or watch
a silent barge come clear of bridges
settling their reflections in the blue canal.

Andrew Motion

✤ *Write your own response to the picture, or to another familiar building whose history you know. Perhaps there is a memorial in your neighbourhood which inspires strong feelings in you when you see or visit it.*

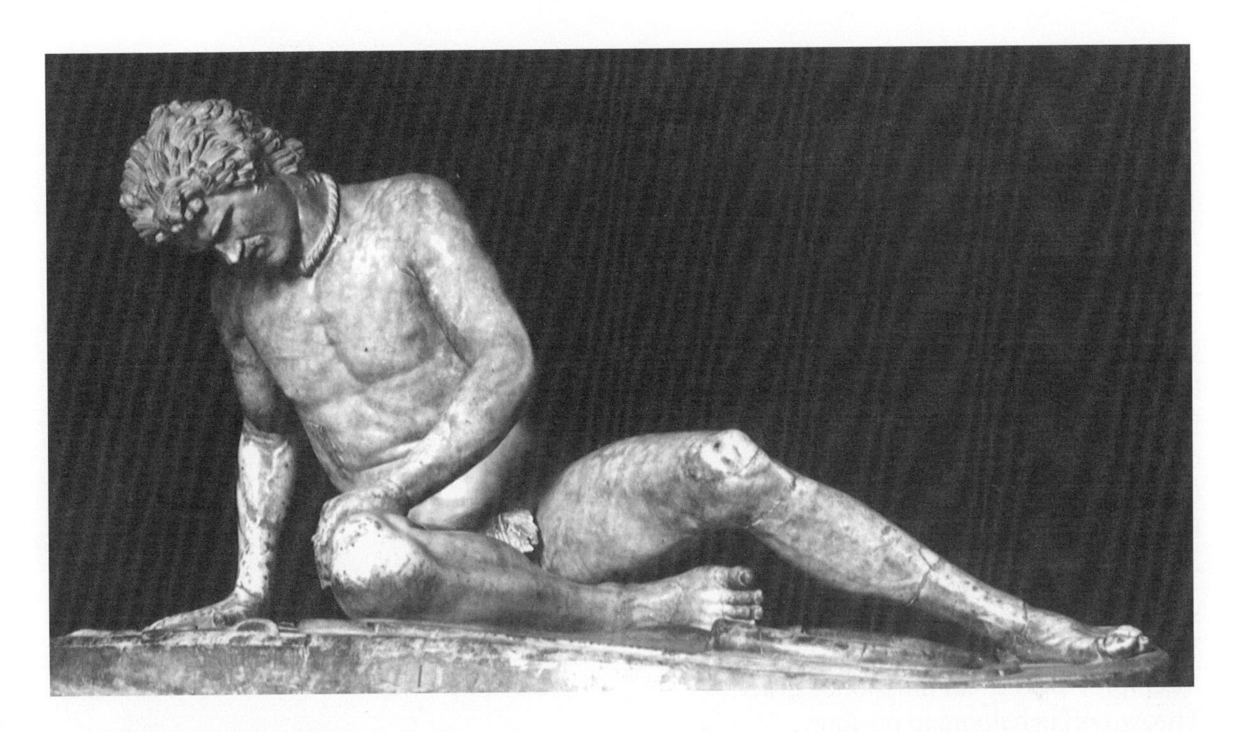

The Dying Gladiator

Gladiators used to fight in Roman amphitheatres as much for the entertainment of the Romans as for their own survival. What feelings does this poem move in you? Think about the destruction of a life for the entertainment of others.

I see before me the Gladiator lie:
He leans upon his hand – his manly brow
Consents to death, but conquers agony,
And his drooped head sinks gradually low –
And through his side the last drops, ebbing slow
From the red gash, fall heavy, one by one,
Like the first of a thunder-shower; and now
The arena swims around him – he is gone,
Ere ceased the inhuman shout which hailed the wretch
who won.

He heard it, but he heeded not – his eyes
Were with his heart and that was far away;
He recked not of the life he lost nor prize,
But where his rude hut by the Danube lay,
There were his young barbarians all at play,
There was their Dacian mother – he, their sire,
Butchered to make a Roman holiday –
All this rushed with his blood – Shall he expire
And unavenged? – Arise! ye Goths, and glut your ire!

Lord Byron

'In composition I do not think second thoughts are best.'
Lord Byron

An Arundel Tomb

Side by side, their faces blurred,
The earl and countess lie in stone,
Their proper habits vaguely shown
As jointed armour, stiffened pleat,
And that faint hint of the absurd –
The little dogs under their feet.

Such plainness of the pre-baroque
Hardly involves the eye, until
It meets his left-hand gauntlet, still
Clasped empty in the other; and
One sees, with a sharp tender shock,
His hand withdrawn, holding her hand.

They would not think to lie so long.
Such faithfulness in effigy
Was just a detail friends would see:
A sculptor's sweet commissioned grace
Thrown off in helping to prolong
The Latin names around the base.

They would not guess how early in
Their supine stationary voyage
The air would change to soundless damage,
Turn the old tenantry away;
How soon succeeding eyes begin
To look, not read. Rigidly they

Persisted, linked, through lengths and breadths
Of time. Snow fell, undated. Light
Each summer thronged the glass. A bright
Litter of birdcalls strewed the same
Bone-riddled ground. And up the paths
The endless altered people came,

Washing at their identity.
Now, helpless in the hollow of
An unarmorial age, a trough
Of smoke in slow suspended skeins
Above their scrap of history,
Only an attitude remains:

Time has transfigured them into
Untruth. The stone fidelity
They hardly meant has come to be
Their final blazon, and to prove
Our almost-instinct almost true:
What will survive of us is love.

Philip Larkin

Notice the regular rhyme scheme in this poem (see page 63 on **rhyme***). Philip Larkin has allowed the memories implied by an historic tomb to bring ideas to his mind; he has focused on one tomb in the church, that of an earl and countess lying side by side, and imagines their life together in Arundel, in Sussex.*

✤ *Write your own response to a tomb; or after a visit to your local church imagine events behind the death of some of those buried there.*

'Usually the idea of a poem comes with a line or two of it, and they determine the rest.'

Philip Larkin

Abbey Tomb

I told them not to ring the bells
The night the Vikings came
Out of the sea and passed us by.
The fog was thick as cream
And in the abbey we stood still
As if our breath might blare
Or pulses rattle if we once
Stopped staring at the door.

Through the walls and through the fog
We heard them passing by.
The deafer monks thanked God too soon
And later only I
Could catch the sound of prowling men
Still present in the hills
So everybody else agreed
To ring the abbey bells.

And even while the final clang
Still snored upon the air,
And while the ringers joked their way
Down round the spiral stair,
Before the spit of fervent prayer
Had dried into the stone
The raiders came back through the fog
And killed us one by one.

Father Abbot at the altar
Lay back with his knees
Doubled under him, caught napping
In the act of praise.
Brother John lay unresponsive
In the warming room.
The spiders came out for the heat
And then the rats for him.

Under the level of the sheep
Who graze here all the time
We lie now, under tourists' feet
Who in good weather come.
I told them not to ring the bells
But centuries of rain
And blustering have made their tombs
Look just as right as mine.

Patricia Beer

In this poem, Patricia Beer has allowed the dead stones of an abbey to come to life in her imagination and take her back into the past.

> *'We all tended to hide our feelings (at school in the 1930s) ... A poem that dealt with what we really felt was quite out of the question.'*
>
> *Patricia Beer*

On Looking at Stubbs's 'Anatomy of the Horse'

In Lincolnshire, a village full of tongues
Not tired by a year's wagging, and a man
Shut in a room where a wrecked carcass hangs,
His calm knife peeling putrid flesh from bone.
He whistles softly, as an ostler would;
The dead horse moves, as if it understood.

That night a yokel holds the taproom still
With tales new-hatched; he's peeped, and seen a mare
Stand there alive with naked rib and skull –
The creature neighed, and stamped upon the floor;
The warlock asked her questions, and she spoke;
He wrote her answers down in a huge book.

Two centuries gone, I have the folio here,
And turn the pages, find them pitiless.
These charts of sinew, vein and bone require
A glance more expert, more detached than this –
Fingering the margins, I think of the old
Sway-backed and broken nags the pictures killed.

Yet, standing in that room, I watch the knife;
Light dances on it as it maps a joint
Or scribes a muscle; I am blank and stiff
The blade cuts so directly to my want;
I gape for anecdote, absurd detail,
Like any yokel with his pint of ale.

Edward Lucie-Smith

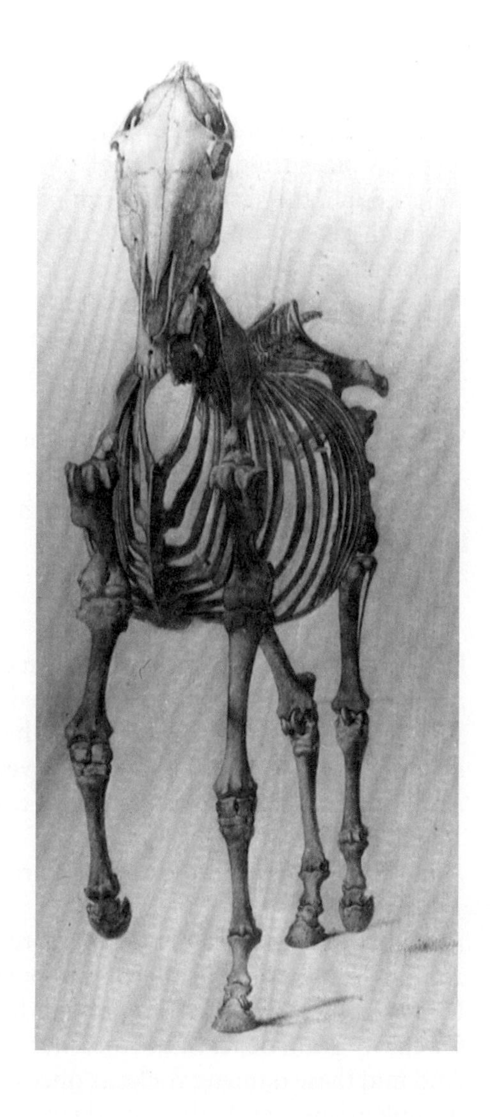

George Stubbs's series of rather clinical illustrations has aroused vivid responses in this poet. Studying anatomy involves literally getting 'down to the bones' of a creature.

❖ *Write your own poetic response to this skeleton, or to an imaginary one.*

Kubla Khan

In Xanadu did Kubla Khan
A stately pleasure-dome decree:
Where Alph, the sacred river, ran
Through caverns measureless to man
Down to a sunless sea.
So twice five miles of fertile ground
With walls and towers were girdled round:
And there were gardens bright with sinuous rills
Where blossom'd many an incense-bearing tree;
And here were forests ancient as the hills,
Enfolding sunny spots of greenery.

But oh, that deep romantic chasm which slanted
Down the green hill athwart a cedarn cover!
A savage place! as holy and enchanted
As e'er beneath a waning moon was haunted
By woman wailing for her demon-lover!
And from this chasm, with ceaseless turmoil seething,
As if this earth in fast thick pants were breathing,
A mighty fountain momently was forced:
Amid whose swift half-intermitted burst
Huge fragments vaulted like rebounding hail,
Or chaffy grain beneath the thresher's flail:
And mid these dancing rocks at once and ever
It flung up momently the sacred river.
Five miles meandering with a mazy motion
Through wood and dale the sacred river ran,
Then reach'd the caverns measureless to man,
And sank in tumult to a lifeless ocean:
And 'mid this tumult Kubla heard from far
Ancestral voices prophesying war!

The shadow of the dome of pleasure
Floated midway on the waves;
Where was heard the mingled measure
From the fountain and the caves.
It was a miracle of rare device,
A sunny pleasure-dome with caves of ice!

A damsel with a dulcimer
In a vision once I saw:
It was an Abyssinian maid,
And on her dulcimer she play'd,
Singing of Mount Abora.
Could I revive within me
Her symphony and song,
To such a deep delight 'twould win me,
That with music loud and long,
I would build that dome in air,
That sunny dome! those caves of ice!
And all who heard should see them there,
And all should cry, Beware! Beware!
His flashing eyes, his floating hair!
Weave a circle round him thrice,
And close your eyes with holy dread,
For he on honey-dew hath fed,
And drunk the milk of Paradise.

Samuel Taylor Coleridge

***Kubla Khan** is explained by Coleridge in the following extract from his writings, and is well known as a poem of fantasy, perhaps brought on by drug-induced sleep.*

✤ *Try your own fantasy poem, beginning with,*

In a vision once I saw . . .

Kubla Khan

Or, A Vision in a Dream. A Fragment.

The following fragment is here published at the request of a poet of great and deserved celebrity [Lord Byron], and, as far as the Author's own opinions are concerned, rather as a psychological curiosity, than on the ground of any supposed poetic merits.

In the summer of the year 1797, the Author, then in ill health, had retired to a lonely farm-house between Porlock and Linton, on the Exmoor confines of Somerset and Devonshire. In consequence of a slight indisposition, an anodyne had been prescribed, from the effects of which he fell asleep in his chair at the moment that he was reading the following sentence, or words of the same substance, in 'Purchas's Pilgrimage': 'Here the Khan Kubla commanded a palace to be built, and a stately garden thereunto. And thus ten miles of fertile ground were inclosed with a wall.' The Author continued for about three hours in a profound sleep, at least of the external senses, during which time he has the most vivid confidence, that he could not have composed less than two to three hundred lines; if that indeed can be called composition in which all the images rose up before him as things, with a parallel production of the correspondent expressions, without any sensation or consciousness of effort. On awaking he appeared to himself to have a distinct recollection of the whole, and taking his pen, ink, and paper, instantly and eagerly wrote down the lines that are here preserved. At this moment he was unfortunately called out by a person on business from Porlock, and detained by him above an hour, and on his return to his room, found, to his no small surprise and mortification, that though he still retained some vague and dim recollection of the general purport of the vision, yet, with the exception of some eight or ten scattered lines and images, all the rest had passed away like the images on the surface of a stream into which a stone has been cast, but, alas! without the after restoration of the latter!

'Poetry – the best words in the best order.'
Samuel Taylor Coleridge

Musée des Beaux Arts

About suffering they were never wrong,
The Old Masters: how well they understood
Its human position; how it takes place
While someone else is eating or opening a window or just walking dully along;
How, when the aged are reverently, passionately waiting
For the miraculous birth, there always must be
Children who did not specially want it to happen, skating
On a pond at the edge of the wood:
They never forgot
That even the dreadful martyrdom must run its course
Anyhow in a corner, some untidy spot
Where the dogs go on with their doggy life and the torturer's horse
Scratches its innocent behind on a tree.
In Breughel's *Icarus*, for instance: how everything turns away
Quite leisurely from the disaster; the ploughman may
Have heard the splash, the forsaken cry,
But for him it was not an important failure; the sun shone
As it had to on the white legs disappearing into the green
Water; and the expensive delicate ship that must have seen
Something amazing, a boy falling out of the sky,
Had somewhere to get to and sailed calmly on.

W. H. Auden

In classical mythology, Icarus, with the help of his father Daedalus, tried to fly by fixing birds' wings to his shoulders with wax. He flew too near the sun, the wax melted, and he fell into the sea. In Breughel's famous painting, 'The Fall of Icarus', it takes a careful eye to find the main figure of the title. In his poem, the poet Auden considers the artist's perspective in this picture.

✤ *Write your own poem arising from a study of this picture.*

> *'In poetry you have a form looking for a subject and a subject looking for a form. When they come together successfully you have a poem.'*
>
> W. H. Auden

This Poem . . .

This poem is dangerous: it should not be left
Within the reach of children, or even of adults
Who might swallow it whole, with possibly
Undesirable side-effects. If you come across
An unattended, unidentified poem
In a public place, do not attempt to tackle it
Yourself. Send it (preferably, in a sealed container)
To the nearest centre of learning, where it will be rendered
Harmless, by experts. Even the simplest poem
May destroy your immunity to human emotions.
All poems must carry a Government warning. Words
Can seriously affect your heart.

Elma Mitchell

Acknowledgements

The publishers would like to thank the following for permission to reproduce photographs and other copyright material:

p.12: T. Phillips, 'William Blake', 1807, National Portrait Gallery, London; p.14 top and bottom, p.18 right: manuscripts from 'Songs of Innocence and Experience' by William Blake, British Library; p.37: B.R. Haydon, 'William Wordsworth', 1818, National Portrait Gallery, London; p.61: manuscript of 'Stopping by Woods on a Snowy Evening', Estate of Robert Frost; p.64: M. Hubrecht, 'D.H. Lawrence', 1920–21, National Portrait Gallery, London; p.81: Roger McGough/McCaw Arts; p.84: Roger McGough, 'The Birderman'; p.88: Sir John E. Millais, 'The Boyhood of Raleigh', Tate Gallery, London; p.106: Ken Bray; p.107: Arnold Stein; p.108 top: sketch by Arnold Stein; p.121: manuscript of 'Ozymandias' by Percy Bysshe Shelley, Bodleian Library, Oxford; p.132: U.A. Fanthorpe; p.137: Uccello, 'St. George and the Dragon', National Gallery, London; p.142: Anne Frank Stichtung; p.143: Museo Capitolino, Rome/Anderson/Mansell Collection; p.145: A.F. Kirsting; p.147: George Stubbs, drawing from 'The Anatomy of the Horse', Royal Academy of Arts, London; p.151: Breughel, 'The Fall of Icarus', Musées Royaux des Beaux Arts de Belgique.

The editors and publisher are grateful for permission to include the following copyright poems:

Fleur Adcock, 'Accidents' from The Incident Book (OUP 1986), © Fleur Adcock 1986. Reprinted by permission of Oxford University Press. W H Auden, 'Musee des Beaux Arts' from Collected Shorter Poems. Reprinted by permission of Faber & Faber Ltd. Elizabeth Bartlett, 'Charlotte, Her Book' from Strange Territory (Peterloo Poets, 1983). Reprinted by permission of the publisher. Patricia Beer, 'Abbey Tomb' and 'After Death' from Just Like the Resurrection. Reprinted by permission of the author. James Berry, 'Spite Shots Labels' and 'Seeing Granny' from When I Dance (Hamish Hamilton Children's Books, 1988) copyright © James Berry, 1988. Reprinted by permission of Hamish Hamilton Ltd. John Betjeman, extracts from Summoned By Bells. Reprinted by permission of John Murray (Publishers) Ltd. G F Bradby, 'April'. Reprinted by permission of Edward Bradby and Anne Ridler. Charles Causley, 'Ballad of the Faithless Wife' and 'School at 4 O'Clock' from Collected Poems (Macmillan). Reprinted by permission of David Higham Associates Ltd. Gillian Clarke, 'Scything' from Letter from A Far Country. Reprinted by permission of Carcanet Press Limited. 'Babysitting' from The Sundial. Reprinted by permission of Gomer Press. Wendy Cope, 'Pastoral' and 'An Argument with Wordsworth'. Both copyright Wendy Cope and reprinted with her permission. Jeni Couzyn, 'Graces' ('Grace for Potato', 'Grace for Snow' and 'Grace for Tomato') reprinted from Christmas in Africa (Heinemann). © Jeni Couzyn 1975. Reprinted by permission of the author. 'Grace for Potato' is also in Life By Drowning: Selected Poems (Bloodaxe Books), © 1985, 1990 Jeni Couzyn. e e cummings, 'who knows if the moon's a balloon' from Complete Poems. Reprinted by permission of Granada/Grafton, part of HarperCollins Publishers. Walter de la Mare, 'Dry August Burned'. Reprinted by permission of The Literary Trustees of Walter de la Mare and The Society of Authors as their representative. Emily Dickinson, Poem # 875 ('I stepped from Plank to Plank') and 444 ('It feels a shame to be Alive'), from The Complete Poems of Emily Dickinson, edited by Thomas H Johnson, copyright 1929 by Martha Dickinson Bianchi, © renewed 1957 by Mary L Hampson, and reprinted by permission of the publishers and the Trustees of Amherst College from The Poems of Emily Dickinson, edited by Thomas H Johnson, Cambridge, Mass: The Belknap Press of Harvard University Press, Copyright 1951, © 1955, 1979, 1983 by the President and Fellows of Harvard College. Keith Douglas, 'Vergissmeinnicht' (and draft) from The Complete Poems of Keith Douglas, edited by Desmond Graham (OUP 1978), © Marie J Douglas 1978. Reprinted by permission of Oxford University Press. Douglas Dunn, 'A Removal from Terry Street', 'Men of Terry Street' and 'War Blinded' from Selected Poems 1964–83. Reprinted by permission of Faber & Faber Ltd. Steve Ellis, 'St Francis's "Cantico di frate sole"

Acknowledgements *continued*

done in Hollywood gangsterese' from Home and Away (Bloodaxe Books, 1987). Reprinted by permission of Bloodaxe Books Ltd. U A Fanthorpe, 'Not my best side' and 'Patience Strong' from Side Effects (Peterloo Poets, 1978); 'Children Imagining a Hospital', Commissioned by Cheltenham Literary Festival, reprinted in First and Always, comp. & ed. Lawrence Sail (Faber, 1988); 'Our Dog Chasing Swifts' from Splinters (OUP, 1988); 'You will be hearing from us', 'Reindeer Report' and 'BC : AD' from Standing To (Peterloo Poets, 1982); 'Swifts', copyright U A Fanthorpe; 'Knowing About Sonnets' from Voices Off (Peterloo Poets, 1984); 'Dear Mr Lee', Commissioned by Wishing Well Appeal, Gt. Ormond St Children's Hospital, reprinted in A Watching Brief (Peterloo Poets, 1987). All reprinted by permission of the author. Robert Frost, 'Beyond Words', 'Mending Wall' and 'Stopping By Woods on a Snowy Evening' from The Poetry of Robert Frost, edited by Edward Connery Lathem. Reprinted by permission of the Estate of Robert Frost and Jonathan Cape Ltd, Publisher. Angie Gilligan, 'Household Dilemma' from New British Poetry. Reprinted by permission of Grafton Books, part of HarperCollins Publishers. Philip Gross, 'Nursery Rhymes' and 'The Ice Factory' from Familiars (Peterloo Poets, 1983). Reprinted by permission of the publishers. Arthur Guiterman, 'Sea-Chill' from Gaily the Troubadour (E P Dutton). Reprinted by permission of Louise H Sclove, New York. Seamus Heaney, 'Follower' from Death of a Naturalist. Reprinted by permission of Faber & Faber Ltd. John Heath-Stubbs, 'Eleven Pipers Piping' from A Partridge in a Pear Tree (Hearing Eye). Reprinted by permission of David Higham Associates Ltd. Teresa Hooley, 'A War Film' from Songs for all Seasons. Reprinted by permission of Jonathan Cape Ltd, Publisher, on behalf of the author. Libby Houston, 'Post-War', first published in A Stained Glass Raree Show (Allison & Busby Ltd, 1967). © Libby Houston 1967. Reprinted by permission of the author. Ted Hughes, 'October Dawn' from The Hawk in the Rain and 'Relic' from Lupercal. Reprinted by permission of Faber & Faber Ltd. David Jacobs, 'Pioneers' and 'The White Flag' from Haarlem Road (Peterloo Poets, 1988). Reprinted by permission of the publisher. Elizabeth Jennings, 'The Prodigal Son' from Tributes (Carcanet). Reprinted by permission of David Higham Associates Ltd. Philip Larkin, 'The Mower', 'Days' and 'An Arundel Tomb' from Collected Poems. Reprinted by permission of Faber & Faber Ltd. Edward Lucie-Smith, 'On Looking at Stubb's "Anatomy of the Horse"' from A Tropical Childhood (OUP, 1961). Reprinted by permission of Rogers Coleridge and White Ltd. Norman MacCaig, 'Neighbour' from Neighbours (Peterloo Poets). Reprinted by permission of the author. 'Thorns' and 'Interruption to a Journey' from Collected Poems. Reprinted by permission of Chatto & Windus, Publishers on behalf of the author. Louis MacNeice, 'Autobiography' from Collected Poems (Faber). Reprinted by permission of David Higham Associates Ltd. John Masefield, 'Sea-Fever'. Reprinted by permission of The Society of Authors as the literary representative of the Estate of John Masefield. Gerda Mayer, 'Make Believe' first on Poetry Now (BBC, Radio 3 1987), 'Postcard in Pen and Ink, 1916', first published in Writing Women (1983) and 'The Seven', first published in The Honest Ulsterman (1982), all from Heartache of Grass (Peterloo Poets, 1988); 'Babes in the Wood', first published in The Poetry Review (1969); 'The Hansel and Gretel House' and 'A Lion, A Wolf and a Fox', first published in Meridian (1974), all from The Candy-Floss Tree (OUP, 1984); 'The Man on the Desert Island' first published in And 3 (1963), and '529 1983', both from The Knockabout Show (Chatto, 1978); 'Tony Douglas Was the Best', first published in Priapus (1970), from Monkey on the Analyst's Couch (Ceolfrith Press, 1980). All reprinted by permission of the author. Roger McGough, 'The Boyhood of Raleigh', 'A Cautionary Calendar', 'Hearts and Flowers' and 'Tramp, Tramp, Tramp' from Melting Into the Foreground (Penguin); 'The Examination' and 'The Birderman' from Waving at Trains (Penguin); 'Hundreds and Thousands' from Nailing the Shadow (Penguin) and 'The Identification' from The Mersey Sound Vol. 2 (Penguin). All reprinted by permission of the Peters Fraser & Dunlop Group Ltd. Edna St Vincent Millay, 'Conscientious Objector' from Collected Poems

(Harper & Row). Copyright 1934, © 1962 by Edna St Vincent Millay and Norma Millay Ellis. Reprinted by permission of Elizabeth Barnett, Literary Executor. Adrian Mitchell, 'A Man May Be Happy' from Love Songs of World War Three, *'Old Age Report', 'The First Journey' and 'Song in Space' from* Nothingmas Day. *Reprinted by permission of the author.* ***NB: These poems should not be used in connection with any examination or test whatsoever.*** *Elma Mitchell, 'This Poem ...' from* People Etcetera *(Peterloo Poets, 1987). Reprinted by permission of the publisher. Andrew Motion, 'Anne Frank Huis' from* Dangerous Play. *Reprinted by permission of the author. Paul Muldoon, 'Why Brownlee Left' from* Why Brownlee Left. *Reprinted by permission of Faber & Faber Ltd. Grace Nichols, 'Like a Beacon' from* The Fat Black Woman's Poems. *Reprinted by permission of Virago Press. Norman Nicholson, 'Wall' from* Sea to the West *(Faber). Reprinted by permission of David Higham Associates Ltd. Wilfred Owen, 'Futility' drafts from* Wilfred Owen: The Complete Poems and Fragments, *ed. Jon Stallworthy. Reprinted by permission of Random Century Group on behalf of the Estate of Wilfred Owen and The Hogarth Press as publishers. Brian Patten, 'Little Johnny's Final Letter' from* Little Johnny's Confession and 'The Projectionist's Nightmare' from Notes to a Hurrying Man. *Reprinted* by permission of Rogers Coleridge and White Ltd. Craig Raine, 'A Martian Sends a Postcard Home' from A Martian Sends a Postcard Home *(OUP 1979), © Craig Raine 1979. Reprinted by permission of Oxford University Press. Kathleen Raine, 'The Moment' from* Collected Poems 1935–80. *Reprinted by permission of Unwin Hyman, part of HarperCollins Publishers. Siegfried Sassoon, 'Base Details', 'The General' and 'The Dug-Out'. Reprinted by permission of George Sassoon. Stevie Smith, 'The Jungle Husband' and 'The River God' from* The Collected Poems of Stevie Smith *(Penguin 20th Century Classics). Reprinted by permission of James MacGibbon, Literary Executor. Stephen Spender, 'Ultima Ratio Regum' from* Collected Poems 1928–53. *Reprinted by permission of Faber & Faber Ltd. Jon Stallworthy, extract from 'The Almond Tree' from* Root and Branch. *Reprinted by permission of Chatto & Windus, Publisher, on behalf of the author. Dylan Thomas, 'Fern Hill' and 'Do Not Go Gentle Into That Good Night' from* The Poems *(J M Dent). Reprinted by permission of David Higham Associates Ltd. R S Thomas, 'The Poacher' from* Song at the Year's Turning *(Rupert Hart-Davis, London 1955). © R S Thomas. Used with permission. Andrew Young, 'The Fairy Ring' from* The Poetical Works of Andrew Young *(Secker & Warburg). Reprinted by permission of Alison Lowbury.*

Index *of titles and first lines (first lines are in light type)*

Index continued

Index continued

Index *continued*